This book is from
the kitchen library of

_____

_____

Art Ginsburg
Mr. Food®

WILLIAM MORROW AND COMPANY, INC.
NEW YORK

Library of Congress Cataloging-in-Publication Data

Ginsburg, Art.
    Mr. Food's restaurant favorites / Art Ginsburg.—1st. ed.
        p.   cm.
    ISBN 0-688-15680-0
    1. Cookery.   I. Title.
TX714.G5734   1999
641.5—dc21   99-36710
                                                          CIP

Printed in the United States of America

First Edition

1   2   3   4   5   6   7   8   9   10

BOOK DESIGN BY MICHAEL MENDELSOHN OF MM DESIGN 2000, INC.

www.williammorrow.com
www.mrfood.com

ACKNOWLEDGMENTS

No matter what or where we're eating, whether it's fancy or down-home, in a grand ballroom or Mom's kitchen, one of the best parts of a meal is the company we share it with. And, really, that's true for almost everything we do. That's why it's so important to me to thank all the people who've helped me put together this cookbook full of restaurant favorites.

At a restaurant, we're given a menu full of choices, and, similarly, I've got a menu of terrific test-kitchen staff who helped me tinker with all the recipes in this book, from the beginning until we got 'em just right: Patty Rosenthal, Janice Bruce, Cheryl Gerber, Cela Goodhue, and Gerri Seinberg. They, along with Joe Peppi, who oversees all the kitchen details plus many aspects of production for my TV show, really live up to the idea of fine company no matter how you look at it! And that's also true of Dio Gomez, who keeps the kitchen bright and clean, and Ginny Lalka, who documents all our recipe successes.

And once we've got the results we're looking for, we need to serve them up, well, if not on a silver platter, then at least in an easy-to-use cookbook! The always creative Howard Rosenthal and Caryl Ginsburg Fantel, with assistants Larissa Lalka and Rhonda Weiss, have packaged it all "to go" for you, so that you can enjoy making and eating these dishes as much as we have!

Following all this creative fun, there's still the time for serious business. Just as every restaurant needs a good manager to keep everything running smoothly, I've got a dynamic group of managers who, along with Caryl and Howard, keep it all going smoothly for me: Steve

Ginsburg, Chet Rosenbaum, and Tom Palombo, and office staff Carol
Ginsburg, Alice Palombo, Ivone Sousa, Beth Ives, and Robin Steiner
do a great job with our 160-plus TV stations, associations with food
councils and companies, and other assorted matters. Helayne
Rosenblum, my script assistant, continues to help me deliver lots of
good taste to you on my daily TV segments, while my assistant Marilyn
Ruderman keeps me organized no matter how busy my schedule is.
Wow, what a plateful!

And, speaking of being busy, my wife Ethel sure is, yet she's still
always there when I need her, along with my son Chuck and the rest of
my family.

Yes, I'm lucky to have lots of good company, because, along with
everyone I've just mentioned, there's also my agent, Bill Adler, and all
the wonderful people at publisher William Morrow, especially Michael
Murphy, publisher and senior vice president; senior editor Zachary
Schisgal; art director Richard Aquan; Nikki Basilone, vice president
and director of special sales; Patrick Jennings, special sales manager;
and, of course, my terrific book designer, Michael Mendelsohn of MM
Design 2000, Inc.

Yup, there's no doubt about it—whether we're working, playing, or
eating—it's the special people in our lives who make our experiences
enjoyable. That's why, when I think of all the places I've eaten—from
fancy restaurants to my own kitchen—and all the super recipes in this
cookbook, I can't keep from thinking about (and thanking!) all these
wonderful people, plus you, my loyal fans, for helping me and inspiring
me to create so many reasons for us all to say, "OOH IT'S SO GOOD!!®"

CONTENTS

INTRODUCTION

I'm so excited! I finally get to share my all-time favorite restaurant foods with you! Everybody has a restaurant favorite—or two or three—but what so many people don't know is that they can make and enjoy restaurant classics right in their own kitchens . . . without spending hours preparing or having to run around to fancy gourmet stores. That's 'cause these recipes (like **all** Mr. Food recipes) are quick and easy and have ingredients we can find at our local supermarkets.

You know, it seems like I've been working on this book for years. Not only has every recipe here been tested and tasted again and again in my test kitchen, but they are based on actual dishes I've enjoyed in restaurants all around the country.

You can probably guess that I travel a lot . . . a whole lot. And with all my TV markets spread throughout the country, my travels have given me the chance to meet loads of super people while offering me the tasty opportunity to dine in many different restaurants. In fact, over the years I've eaten in so many that I sometimes refer to restaurants as my homes away from home—from neighborhood mom-and-pop eateries and local diners to four-star gourmet restaurants, and everything in between!

Of course, I've done more than just sit and enjoy my food at these restaurants! I've managed to sneak into a kitchen or two to talk with the chefs, cooks, and owners and pick up a load of helpful hints. Believe it or not, professional cooks don't always use complicated techniques that take years to perfect. Uh uh! They often use shortcuts that are simple enough for anybody to do.

So, armed with years of experience as a butcher, caterer, and food fanatic, I've taken these great tips and mixed them with a heaping dose of my practical food preparation philosophy to make these popular recipes as easy as can be so that anybody—even those of us with hectic schedules—can enjoy making and eating their restaurant favorites right at home . . . for a whole lot less!

And this book has everything, so get all spiffed up and enjoy a gourmet-tasting meal of Jumbo Shrimp Cocktail, Classic Filet Mignon, Potatoes Lyonnaise, Asparagus with Hollandaise Sauce, and Rich Chocolate Mousse. Or dress down and enjoy yummy favorites such as Buffalo Wings and Chicago Deep-dish Pizza, or Mr. Food's Fast Burgers and Baked Sweet Potato Fries. Yup, they're all ready in no time. You can even enjoy Greek and Italian dishes, and lots of other ethnic specialties in just minutes, too. And the best part? There's no tipping required!

From now on, eating restaurant-style food at home won't necessarily mean calling for takeout. Now that you've got Mr. Food's Restaurant Favorites, every night's menu will be packed with lots of "OOH IT'S SO GOOD!!®"

"Menuology": A Fun and Easy-to-Understand Guide to Common Restaurant Terms

à la carte—a menu where each item is priced separately

à la king—a preparation made with a white cream sauce traditionally containing mushrooms, green peppers, and pimientos

à la mode—refers to ice cream served over or alongside another item, like a piece of pie or hunk of brownie

al dente—means "to the tooth" in Italian and refers to pasta that has been cooked to the point where it has a slight bit of uncooked core, so it's still chewy instead of totally limp

appetizers—snacks served with beverages before a meal. These are what I like to refer to as predinner munchies. Oh—don't eat too many appetizers or you won't have room for your entrée!

aspic—a jellied dish or jellied glaze

au gratin—a baked dish most commonly topped with crumbs and cheese then top-browned. Most of us are familiar with potatoes prepared this way.

au jus—natural juices, drippings, or gravy most commonly served with prime rib

bain-marie—often used at buffets, it's a steam table with cutouts for holding pans of food at desired temperatures.

baste—the process of moistening food with water, drippings, or seasoned sauce while it's cooking to keep it from drying out or burning. This one little word is the reason most pot roasts and turkeys have that melt-in-your-mouth flavor.

beurre—French for butter

blacken—we have chef Paul Prudhomme of K-Paul's restaurant in New Orleans to thank for this cooking method where an item is coated with a seasoning blend and seared in an extremely hot pan over high heat until black on the outside

blend—to thoroughly mix two or more ingredients

bisque—a thick cream soup usually made with seafood

bon appétit—literally means "good appetite" and is said when wishing for someone to enjoy his meal

bordelaise—a brown sauce made with red wine, shallots, lemon juice, pepper, and thyme (originally made with red wine from Bordeaux, France—that's how it got its name)

bouquet garni—a mixture of herbs tied together in cheesecloth and used to flavor soups and sauces. Don't forget to remove it before serving or you're likely to end up with a spoonful of cloth instead of soup.

braise—to brown food such as pot roast, then cook it slowly in a small amount of liquid

braten—a German marinated pot roast usually cooked in a small amount of liquid on the stovetop

broil—to cook food by exposing it to extreme direct heat

buffet—a display of ready-to-eat foods to which patrons help themselves

burrito—a soft flour tortilla wrapped around a meat, chicken, cheese, or bean filling

bus—to clear a dining table and possibly also assist a waiter by filling beverage orders for diners

calzone—an Italian turnover stuffed with ingredients that you'd find on pizza *canapé*—an appetizer of a small piece of toasted or fried bread topped with a flavorful spread and, typically, garnished

cappuccino—a hot drink made with very strong coffee (espresso) and hot steamed milk, and often topped with cinnamon

carne—Spanish for meat, as in the dish chili con carne

caviar—the roe (eggs) of sturgeon and salmon; considered a pricey delicacy

chef—the person in authority in a kitchen. The chef has complete control of all food preparation and also supervises the serving of food. He/she may also be known as the executive chef or head chef. You can generally identify a chef by his/her tall white hat.

chop—to cut food into small pieces with a knife, cleaver, or other utensil. Also, a cut of meat with a bone still attached, as in a lamb chop.

chorizo—a Spanish type of pork sausage that's made with paprika (which gives it its bright red color)

cilantro—the fresh form of coriander, this leafy flavoring is popular in Spanish and Latin cooking. As ground coriander, it's used in many Near and Middle Eastern foods.

compote—a stew of fresh or dried fruit (or a combination) in a thick syrup

consommé—a clear broth that may be served plain or used to flavor particular dishes. Yes, it's nothing more than a fancy word for broth.

coquilles—French for seashells; on menus, this is most often used in the dish Coquilles St. Jacques, a baked seafood dish with a cream sauce that is often served in a large seashell

couscous—a Moroccan-style pasta made from semolina wheat; also a dish made with this rice-like grain and chunks of chicken, meat and/or vegetables

crème—French for cream

crêpe—a thin French pancake usually folded or wrapped around a savory or sweet filling *croissant*—a crescent-shaped French pastry roll with rich, flaky, buttery layers

croutons—small cubes of plain or seasoned bread that are toasted or fried and used as a topping for soups and tossed salads

crudités—a selection of cut fresh raw or blanched vegetables served as an hors d'oeuvre with dipping sauces. Remember: Never double-dip your crudité! Because it's unsanitary, it's considered bad manners.

cuisine—a specific cultural style of cooking

dessert—the final course (or the first, depending on how much of a sweet tooth you have) of a meal

diablo/diavolo—Spanish and Italian, respectively, for "devil"; usually refers to a spicy-hot dish

dice—to cut food into small cubes. Omelets are usually filled with diced veggies.

dim sum—steamed dumplings usually filled with ground meats, seafood, or poultry and vegetables; also refers to many different types of Chinese appetizers served together to make a complete meal

drawn butter—unsalted butter that's been melted slowly so that its milk solids can be removed. Also called clarified butter, it is used instead of regular butter for cooking at higher temperatures because it has a higher smoke point.

du jour—French for "of the day," this usually refers to a restaurant's daily special. These items are often prepared in limited quantities and presented on a blackboard or special insert in a restaurant menu. The most common use of this term is soup du jour.

en brochette—something served and/or cooked on a skewer; typically refers to a kebab

en papillote—a cooking method where food is wrapped and baked in a parchment paper casing, most popular with fish or veggies

entrée—in the United States, this generally refers to the main course of a meal

falafel—small fried fritter made of ground garbanzo beans (chickpeas) and typically served on pita bread

filet/fillet—spelled with one *l*, this refers to a long, thin piece of boneless meat, like filet mignon; with two *l*'s, it refers to a long, thin piece of boneless fish or chicken

flambé(e)—fancy restaurants often offer dishes that are laced in spirits and served flaming—yes, flaming! There's a particular way to do this safely, so I advise leaving this one to the pros.

flan—a light egg custard

Florentine—a dish made with spinach

fondue—from the French word for melt, it refers to a melted cheese or chocolate mixture that is served with foods to be dipped in it using long-handled forks or skewers

foo yung—a Chinese omelet made with meat, fish, or vegetables

fraise—French for strawberry

frappé—a semifrozen beverage

fromage—French for cheese. Some people call me the Grand Fromage (the "Big Cheese")

garnish—I like to call this adding pizzazz to a plate before serving. It's easy to do just by adding some carrot or radish flowers or maybe even fresh herbs before serving so that anything you're serving will look as good as it tastes.

Gorgonzola—a very strong Italian blue cheese. (Mmm . . . one of my favorites!)

goulash—a thick meat stew

gravlax—thinly sliced Swedish salmon cured with salt, pepper, sugar, and dill

headwaiter—the waiter who oversees the other waiters. He's the guy to be good to!

hoisin sauce—a popular Chinese sauce used for marinating, cooking, and dipping; made from garlic, hot peppers, soy sauce, and spices

hummus—a spread or dip made of ground garbanzo beans (chickpeas)

julienne—a food item sliced long and thin, almost matchstick size. The most common items to julienne are vegetables, meats, and cheeses for salads and garnishes.

kasha—roasted buckwheat, a grain popular in Russian cooking that is often cooked with mushrooms and onions

kielbasa—traditionally, a spicy beef and pork Polish sausage, although today there are many types, including kosher and light versions made with chicken and turkey

kosher—food that's prepared and served according to set Jewish dietary laws

legume—French for vegetable; in English, it refers mostly to dried peas and beans, the heart of a good minestrone

lyonnaise—anything cooked with onions, most commonly a potato dish

maison—French for house, this is usually used when referring to a dish that's a restaurant's "specialty of the house."

maître d'hôtel (or *maître d'* for short)—the person in charge of a restaurant or catering department. A big tip to him/her will usually get you a desirable table.

marinate—to soak meat, chicken, fish, or veggies in a flavored liquid, called a *marinade*, for a period of time sufficient for it to absorb those flavors. Marinating is most often associated with food that is cooked on a grill.

marzipan—a firm, pliable paste of finely ground almonds, confectioners' sugar, and corn syrup that can be rolled out like pie dough and is often molded into flowers and shapes for decorating fancy pastries and cakes

mein—Chinese for noodles

menu—can mean several things, including a printed list of all the foods served at a particular eating establishment. It can also refer to particular items served; for example, on my family's menu tonight are tossed salad and grilled chicken.

meringue—egg whites whipped with sugar to the stiff-peak stage and usually made into cookies or a pie topping. If you refrigerate meringue it will "weep"—and so will you.

moussaka—a Greek baked dish consisting of layers of eggplant and ground beef topped with a white sauce or a custard *mousse*—a light dessert dish made with whipped cream and flavorings, usually made in a mold and served chilled or frozen

nachos—a Mexican-style appetizer of tortilla chips, chilies, and melted cheese; today it's also popular made with olives, scallions, and other vegetables.

Newburg—a dish made with a sauce of butter, cream, and egg yolks, often served over fresh seafood

paella—a flavorful Spanish stew most often made with chicken, seafood, vegetables, and rice

pain—French for bread

pâté—ground fish, meat, or poultry baked and served chilled as an appetizer

pesto—a sauce of fresh basil, olive oil, garlic, pine (or other) nuts, and grated Parmesan or Romano cheese

phyllo dough—very thin, delicate pastry layers, often found in savory and sweet Greek dishes

pièce de résistance—a very special main-dish food . . . one that usually can't be resisted

poach—a gentle method of preparing eggs, fish, and other foods in a water broth. It's an easy low-fat cooking option.

pomme—French for apple

pomodoro—Italian for tomato

potage—French for soup

poulet—French for chicken

prosciutto—a dried, cured spicy ham (usually quite pricey!)

Provençale—a dish containing tomatoes, onions, bell peppers, garlic, and herbs

purée—food that has been mashed until almost liquefied. We usually purée tomatoes or fruits for sauces, and food is often puréed before serving to babies.

quiche—a savory pie made with cream, cheese, eggs, and vegetables and/or seafood or meats. It's a great choice for brunch or lunch or even cut into squares and served as an hors d'oeuvre.

ragoût—a thick, highly seasoned stew

ratatouille—a mixed vegetable dish that usually includes eggplant, tomatoes, and garlic and is served either warm or cold

rémoulade—a spicy New Orleans–style sauce often served with shrimp or other seafood

risotto—Italian-style rice cooked in broth and, usually, served with cheese

rotisserie—a special device used to broil or barbecue chicken and meats. Rotisserie chicken is a popular take-out item at supermarkets and fast-food restaurants. Mmm, it's a slow cooking method that ensures that foods come out tender and juicy.

roux—a cooked mixture of butter and flour used to thicken soups and sauces

sake—Japanese rice wine

sauté—to cook food in a small amount of fat over high heat until brown on all sides

schnapps—a strong dry liquor available in fruit and other flavors

schnitzel—very thin boneless fillet of sautéed veal, pork, or beef

sear—a cooking technique that browns the surface of meat with high heat, sealing in the juices

smorgasbord—originally referred to a selection of Scandinavian foods, but now refers to any type of hot and cold food served on a buffet table

soufflé—a delicate baked custard that "puffs up" during baking; contains anything from cheese to meat to chocolate. When you've got one of these in the oven, don't slam the oven door or your soufflé will flop!

sous-chef—the second in command in a kitchen, responsible for physical day-to-day kitchen operations and the supervision of kitchen personnel, as well as the preparation of ingredients for use by the chef

steam—to cook veggies, fish, or other food with steam. Watch out for the steam because it's superhot.

steep—this word is most commonly associated with tea. After pouring boiling water over a tea bag, tea should steep (be allowed to sit) for up to five minutes in order to extract the maximum amount of flavor

sushi—a Japanese delight consisting of cold vinegared rice layered or rolled with vegetables, egg, or seafood, most often raw fish; generally served with wasabi (Japanese horseradish), soy sauce, and pickled ginger

taco—a crispy or soft corn tortilla wrapped around a filling of meat, chicken, cheese, or beans

tempura—a lightly battered deep-fried Japanese dish of poultry, seafood, or vegetables, usually served with a selection of dipping sauces. Use chopsticks when eating tempura, 'cause it's real hot.

tip—an amount of money left by a customer as a gratuity to a waiter or bartender for good service. Fifteen percent of a complete meal or beverage check was always considered reasonable, but it's common to reward exceptional service with a twenty percent tip.

toque—the tall brimless hat worn by chefs

truffle—a fancy edible fungus, similar to a mushroom but very pricey, used for seasoning and garnishing. A chocolate truffle is a rich chocolate confection often shaped like a mushroom.

tutti-frutti—mixed fruits

Véronique—made with grapes

vichyssoise—a cream soup made of potatoes and chicken stock that is usually served chilled

vinaigrette—a salad dressing or marinade of oil, vinegar, herbs, and spices

waiter/waitress—a person who serves diners. A waiter or waitress serves as a diner's main contact with the kitchen staff.

Keeping It Light

Some people limit their visits to restaurants—or avoid them completely—because they are watching their waistlines. Well, if that's you, it doesn't have to be a while before you pick up your next menu. That's 'cause I've put together these pointers to help you keep things light:

- When you're out, those sodas, beers, and mixed drinks may sound and taste good, but most of them are full of empty calories. Why waste so much of your daily allotment on drinks? You'll start off ahead if your beverage choice is a refreshing glass of ice water or seltzer with a twist of lemon or lime.
- Request that salad dressings be served on the side, as well as any butter, cheese, or other rich sauces that normally accompany your choice of side dish or main-course items. Having these on the side allows you to dip into them modestly so you can control how much or how little of them you consume.
- It's tempting to dip into the bread basket, so, if you must indulge, have just one serving, and go easy on the toppings.
- Eat slowly. You'll not only enjoy your food more, but you'll give your stomach a chance to send your brain the message that it's full!
- Reduce the size of your portions. You may want to order an appetizer instead of an entrée, or a cup of soup and a bowl of salad instead of a full meal.
- Take your willpower with you to the buffet line. Serve yourself small portions of a few items, then take your time enjoying your choices of lower fat and lower calorie selections like salads, steamed veggies, and grilled meat, chicken, or fish. Don't stuff yourself so much that you need to loosen your belt!
- Split an entrée with a dinner companion. These days, many restaurants serve very large portions—enough to satisfy two

people—so eating a half-sized portion isn't that much of a sacrifice.

- If you can't split an entrée, as soon as you're served, divide it in half and set aside the other half. Ask your server to wrap that second portion so you'll eat only half now and can still have another serving to enjoy the next day for lunch or dinner.
- Most restaurants are willing to alter their menu items slightly in order to meet dietary requirements. For example, you can always ask for the chef to go easy on the cheese melted on your pasta dish or use very little butter if an ingredient is sautéed.
- Ask your server if the chef can poach or grill an item that is typically sautéed or deep-fried. Those are both tasty and low-fat cooking alternatives.
- Check the dessert menu for low-fat options and choose something like ices, sorbet, or fruit salad to satisfy your sweet tooth. Many restaurants now offer these in addition to all those irresistible cakes, pies, and ice cream treats.
- If a rich dessert is a must, order one serving of something that can be shared with a dining companion. Very often, one bite is all it takes to satisfy that end-of-meal craving for something sweet.

A Note About Packaged Foods

Packaged food sizes may vary by brand. Generally, the sizes indicated in these recipes are average sizes. If you can't find the exact package size listed in the ingredients, whatever package is closest in size will usually do the trick.

Golden Stuffed Mushrooms

In my travels I've had occasion to taste many versions of stuffed mushrooms, many of them more than a bit unusual! So when I tried these in a small restaurant in the Midwest, I asked . . . okay, I begged . . . the chef for his secret. It's the corn bread stuffing that puts these mushrooms in a class by themselves.

ABOUT 1 DOZEN MUSHROOMS

1 pound large fresh mushrooms
2 tablespoons butter
¼ cup corn bread stuffing
¼ teaspoon onion powder
⅛ teaspoon salt
⅛ teaspoon black pepper
⅛ teaspoon paprika

Preheat the oven to 375°F. Gently clean the mushrooms by wiping them with a damp paper towel. Remove the stems from ¾ pound of the mushrooms; set aside the caps. Finely chop the stems and the remaining ¼ pound whole mushrooms. Melt the butter in a large skillet over medium heat. Add the chopped mushrooms and cook for 4 to 5 minutes, or until tender. Remove from the heat and add the stuffing, onion powder, salt, and pepper; mix well. Using a teaspoon, stuff the mushroom caps with the stuffing mixture. Place on an ungreased rimmed baking sheet. Sprinkle with the paprika and bake for 10 to 12 minutes, or until heated through. Serve immediately.

Chinese Spareribs

Most people enjoy this staple at Chinese-American restaurants but haven't tried to re-create it in their own kitchens. Well, now's the time to try, 'cause it's easier than you might think. Instead of hanging the ribs while they roast, like the Chinese restaurants do, we'll cook them in the oven for a taste that's almost as rich but just as satisfying.

4 TO 6 SERVINGS

2 cans (10½ ounces each)
   condensed beef broth
½ cup ketchup
½ cup honey
½ cup soy sauce
8 garlic cloves, minced
¼ teaspoon red food color
   (see Tip)
2 teaspoons salt
4 pounds pork spareribs

TIPS FROM THE PROS

Red food color is used to give these ribs their bright color in most Chinese-American restaurants.

In a 9" × 13" baking dish, combine all the ingredients except the ribs; mix well. Add the ribs, turning to coat well with the marinade. Cover and chill for at least 4 hours, or overnight, turning occasionally. Preheat the oven to 450°F. Line a rimmed baking sheet with aluminum foil. Place the ribs on the baking sheet; reserve the marinade for basting. Bake for 15 minutes, then reduce the heat to 350°F. and bake for 1 to 1¼ hours, or until the ribs are tender and the glaze is crispy, basting occasionally with the reserved marinade. Cut into individual ribs and serve.

Jumbo Shrimp Cocktail

I recently had one of the best shrimp cocktails ever. Each shrimp was so firm and full of flavor that I just had to ask the chef for his secret. He whispered to me that he adds a splash of lemon juice to the water when it's boiling and that he keeps the shrimp firm by draining but never rinsing them after boiling. Try it for yourself!

4 TO 6 SERVINGS

8 cups (2 quarts) water
1 small onion, chopped
1 rib celery, chopped
3 tablespoons fresh lemon
    juice, divided
1½ pounds large or colossal
    shrimp, peeled, with tails
    left on, and deveined
1 cup ketchup
3 tablespoons prepared white
    horseradish, drained
2 tablespoons tomato paste

HELPFUL HINTS

The number of servings depends on the size of the shrimp and how many you want to serve per person. There are 12 to 15 jumbo shrimp per pound and 16 to 20 colossal shrimp per pound.

In a soup pot, bring the water, onion, celery, and 2 tablespoons lemon juice to a boil over high heat. Add the shrimp and cook for 2 to 3 minutes, or until the shrimp are pink and cooked through. Drain and chill for at least 2 hours. Meanwhile, in a medium bowl, combine the ketchup, horseradish, tomato paste, and the remaining 1 tablespoon lemon juice; mix well. Cover and chill until ready to serve. Serve the shrimp with the cocktail sauce.

Spring Rolls

Spring rolls are similar to egg rolls, only they're usually a bit lighter and often packed with veggies only—no meat. Why not pick up some egg roll wrappers and make your own version of this quick and tasty snack?

8 SPRING ROLLS

½ cup soy sauce
¼ cup packed light brown sugar
1 tablespoon ground ginger
2 teaspoons garlic powder
6 cups shredded Chinese
   cabbage
2 cups fresh bean sprouts
1 large carrot, shredded
3 scallions, chopped
8 egg roll wrappers
Oil for frying

HELPFUL HINTS

If you serve these with duck sauce or spicy mustard, they'll taste as good as (or better than!) the ones served in restaurants!

HELPFUL HINTS

In a small bowl, combine the soy sauce, brown sugar, ginger, and garlic powder; mix well. In a large bowl, combine the cabbage, bean sprouts, carrot, and scallions; mix well. Pour the soy sauce mixture over the cabbage mixture; toss to coat well and let stand for 10 minutes. Place the cabbage mixture in a colander and squeeze to drain well. Spoon about ½ cup of the cabbage mixture evenly onto the center of each egg roll wrapper. Fold one corner of each egg roll wrapper up over the cabbage mixture, then fold both sides over, envelope fashion; roll up tightly. Heat about 1½ inches oil in a deep medium saucepan over medium-high heat until hot but not smoking. Add the egg rolls in batches and fry for 2 to 3 minutes per side, or until golden. Drain on a paper towel–lined platter. Serve immediately, but be careful—the filling will be hot.

Classic Clams Casino

I've made preparing traditional clams casino even easier than ever. We open the clams by steaming them instead of shucking them raw. Yup, this is how to make restaurant-style clams casino that the whole gang will enjoy, including the chef du jour.

1 DOZEN CLAMS

12 large clams, scrubbed
1 can (4 ounces) mushroom stems and pieces, drained
¾ cup Italian-flavored bread crumbs
½ medium red bell pepper, coarsely chopped
½ medium red onion, coarsely chopped
3 slices bacon

Preheat the oven to 400°F. Fill a large soup pot with 1 inch of water and add the clams. Cover and bring to a boil over high heat; cook for 3 to 5 minutes, or until the clams open. Pull off and discard the top shell of each clam. In a food processor, combine the remaining ingredients and process until smooth. Spoon the bread crumb mixture over the clams and place on a baking sheet. Bake for 25 to 30 minutes, or until lightly browned on top and heated through. Serve immediately.

Hummus Dip

Hummus, once found only in Middle Eastern restaurants, has become a mainstream dish. Loads of restaurants are making it to serve along with pita chips instead of the traditional bread and butter. And now hummus is easier than ever to make at home.

ABOUT 3 CUPS

2 cans (15 ounces each) garbanzo beans (chickpeas), drained, with ⅓ cup liquid reserved

2 garlic cloves

Juice of 1 lemon

3 tablespoons olive oil

1 teaspoon salt

1 teaspoon ground cumin

TIPS FROM THE PROS

You can make this truly Middle Eastern by adding a bit of tahini (sesame seed paste). And why not serve it with pita crisps? They're a snap to make by cutting pita bread into wedges and baking on a baking sheet in a 350°F. oven until crisp.

Combine all the ingredients in a food processor. Process until the mixture is smooth and creamy and no lumps remain, scraping down the sides of the container as needed. Serve immediately, or cover and chill until ready to serve.

Spinach Artichoke Dip

I have a friend who regularly eats at a particular chain restaurant, mostly so she can enjoy their awesome spinach dip appetizer. She always wanted the recipe but couldn't get it, so I went into my test kitchen and came up with a version that rated a "two thumbs up!"

ABOUT 3 CUPS

1 package (10 ounces) frozen
    chopped spinach, thawed
    and squeezed dry
1 package (8 ounces) cream
    cheese, softened
¾ cup grated Parmesan cheese
¼ cup mayonnaise
1 teaspoon fresh lemon juice
¼ teaspoon ground red pepper
¼ teaspoon garlic powder
1 can (14 ounces) artichoke
    hearts, drained and chopped

HELPFUL HINTS
Serve this with a selection of tortilla chips, crackers, or thin slices of French bread for dipping. And to lighten it up, use reduced-fat cream cheese and only ½ cup Parmesan cheese, and serve with baked tortilla chips.

Preheat the oven to 350°F. Coat a 1-quart casserole dish with nonstick cooking spray. In a medium bowl, combine the spinach, cream cheese, Parmesan cheese, mayonnaise, lemon juice, ground red pepper, and garlic powder; beat until well blended. Stir in the artichokes and spoon into the casserole dish. Bake for 30 to 35 minutes, or until heated through and the edges are golden. Serve immediately.

Almond-Crusted Brie

"Fancy schmancy" is what most people think when they see this on a restaurant menu. Usually a dough that's so delicate is difficult to work with. Well, not this one!

---

1 BRIE ROUND

One 8-ounce Brie cheese
   round, well chilled
1 sheet frozen puff pastry
   (from a 17¼-ounce
   package), thawed
1 egg, beaten
2 tablespoons sliced almonds

TIPS FROM THE PROS

You can make this extra special by serving it with wedges of sliced apple, crackers, or thin slices of French bread.

Preheat the oven to 350°F. Place the Brie round in the center of the puff pastry sheet. Bring the edges up to the center, completely covering the Brie; pinch the dough firmly to seal. Trim and discard any excess dough and place seam side down on a large rimmed baking sheet. Brush with the egg and sprinkle with the almonds. Bake for 30 to 35 minutes, or until the cheese is soft and the pastry is golden. Allow to cool slightly before serving.

Buffalo Wings

Lots of restaurants claim that their chicken wings are authentic Buffalo-style wings. If you've ever tried the real ones at the Anchor Bar in Buffalo, New York, you're surely able to judge for yourself. But, for your next get-together, instead of shuffling off to Buffalo, here's how you can whip up some wings that are almost as good as the ones we get there.

ABOUT 4 DOZEN WINGS

1 package (5 pounds) split
   chicken wings, thawed if
   frozen
¾ cup cayenne pepper sauce
½ cup (1 stick) butter, melted

> **TIPS FROM THE PROS**
>
> To be truly authentic Buffalo wings, these wings should be fried in a deep fryer or in a couple inches of hot oil in a soup pot. Fry in batches for about 15 minutes, or until the skin is crispy.

Preheat the oven to 425°F. Place the wings on rimmed baking sheets and bake for 30 minutes. Turn the wings over and bake for 30 more minutes, or until no pink remains and the skin is crispy. In a large plastic container with a tight-fitting lid, combine the cayenne pepper sauce and melted butter; mix well. Add the wings, cover tightly, and shake well. Serve immediately.

NOTE: Make sure to serve these with celery sticks and blue cheese dressing (see page 36), just as they do in Buffalo.

Crispy Bruschetta

*Ever wonder how most restaurants get their garlic bread so crispy? It's easy!
Before toasting it, they spread each piece of bread with a mixture of olive oil
and garlic. It's their little secret for that trendy, flavorful, crispy bruschetta.*

ABOUT 1 DOZEN SLICES

¾ cup olive oil, divided
1½ teaspoons garlic powder,
   divided
1 loaf (16 ounces) Italian or
   French bread, cut into
   1-inch slices
10 plum tomatoes, chopped
¼ cup chopped fresh basil
½ small red onion, finely
   chopped
½ teaspoon salt
¼ teaspoon black pepper

TIPS FROM THE PROS

Baking this in a really hot oven
means the bread gets crispy on the
outside and stays soft on the inside.

Preheat the oven to 400°F. In a small bowl, combine ¼ cup olive oil
and ½ teaspoon garlic powder; mix well and brush over the tops of the
bread slices. Place on a baking sheet and bake for 5 to 6 minutes, or
until golden on both sides. In a large bowl, combine the remaining ½
cup olive oil and 1 teaspoon garlic powder and the remaining ingredients; mix well. Spoon over the toasted bread slices and serve.

Deluxe Antipasto Platter

Antipasto platters, which appear on the menu at just about every Italian restaurant, have always been popular. Sure, each restaurant has its own version, but if you're looking for the one that set the standard . . . this is it!

6 TO 8 SERVINGS

½ pound sliced hard salami

¼ pound sliced capocolla or other spicy ham

6 slices (6 ounces) provolone cheese, cut in half

¼ pound Gorgonzola or other blue cheese, cut into 1-inch cubes

1 can (14 ounces) artichoke hearts, drained and quartered

1 jar (4 ounces) marinated mushrooms, drained

12 peperoncini

¼ pound Sicilian or other green olives, drained

¼ pound Kalamata or other black olives, drained

TIPS FROM THE PROS

If you like greens with your antipasto, prepare this on a bed of mixed salad greens. And you can make it authentic by serving it with crusty Italian bread and roasted garlic.

Arrange the ingredients on a large serving platter as desired, or as follows: Tightly roll the salami slices into tubes and place on the platter. Fold the capocolla slices in half, then in half again, and place on the platter. Arrange the remaining ingredients on the platter and serve.

Layered Nachos Supreme

So many of us go to those trendy restaurants and order nachos supreme, but we never think of making them at home. Well, that's about to change! Now that you know how to prepare restaurant-style nachos, you're gonna be sure to put them on your home dinner menu.

4 TO 6 SERVINGS

1 package (8 ounces) tortilla chips
1 can (16 ounces) refried
   beans
1 envelope (1¼ ounces) taco
   seasoning mix
2 cups (8 ounces) shredded
   Mexican cheese blend
½ cup guacamole
½ cup sour cream
4 scallions, thinly sliced
1 medium tomato, chopped
2 jalapeño peppers, thinly sliced (optional)

TIPS FROM THE PROS

Serve this with salsa and additional guacamole or sour cream on the side.

Preheat the oven to 350°F. Place the tortilla chips in a 9" × 13" baking dish. In a medium saucepan, combine the refried beans and taco seasoning mix over medium heat, stirring constantly until heated through; spoon over the tortilla chips. Sprinkle the cheese over the bean mixture and bake for 3 to 5 minutes, or until the cheese is melted. Dollop with the guacamole and sour cream, then sprinkle with the scallions, tomato, and the sliced jalapeños, if desired. Serve immediately.

SOUPS AND CHOWDERS

Steak House Soup

Steak soup was created by popular steak houses to use up overcooked or left-over steaks. When you think about it, it's an easy way to stretch the taste of our favorite steak dinner into two meals.

6 TO 8 SERVINGS

2 tablespoons vegetable oil

1½ pounds boneless beef top sirloin steak, about ½ inch thick, trimmed and cut into thin strips

½ pound fresh mushrooms, quartered

1 large sweet onion, chopped

4 cups water

3 large potatoes, scrubbed and cut into ½-inch cubes

3 beef bouillon cubes

1 teaspoon ground cumin

½ teaspoon black pepper

2 cups (8 ounces) shredded Monterey Jack cheese

TIPS FROM THE PROS

For a richer, darker soup, stir in some browning and seasoning sauce during the final simmering.

In a soup pot, heat the oil over medium-high heat. Add the steak strips, mushrooms, and onion and cook for 12 to 15 minutes, or until the steak is browned and the onion is tender. Add the remaining ingredients except the cheese and bring to a boil. Reduce the heat to low, cover, and simmer for 25 to 30 minutes, or until the steak and potatoes are tender. Ladle into bowls and serve sprinkled with the shredded cheese.

French Onion Soup

I challenged my test cooks to come up with an easy version of French onion soup that tasted as if it were from a four-star restaurant but didn't take as long to make. They met the challenge in coming up with this one that's sure to earn a four-spoon rating from your gang!

4 TO 6 SERVINGS

3 tablespoons butter
3 large onions, thinly sliced
3 cans (14½ ounces each)
    ready-to-use beef broth
2 bay leaves
¼ teaspoon black pepper
⅓ cup grated Parmesan cheese
⅓ cup dry red wine
Four to six 1-inch-thick slices
    French bread, toasted
½ cup (2 ounces) shredded
    Swiss cheese

TIPS FROM THE PROS

We've simplified the recipe here. Many restaurants make their own broth, then ladle the soup into individual serving bowls and place a toasted slice of French bread in the soup, followed by a slice of Swiss cheese over the top of the bowl, then broil it until the cheese melts.

In a soup pot, melt the butter over medium heat. Add the onions and cook for 25 to 30 minutes, or until golden, stirring occasionally. Add the beef broth, bay leaves, and black pepper and bring to a boil. Preheat the broiler. Reduce the heat under the broth mixture to low; stir in the Parmesan cheese and wine and cook for 3 to 5 minutes, or until the cheese is melted. Meanwhile, place the bread on a broiler pan or baking sheet and sprinkle an equal amount of the Swiss cheese over each slice; broil for 3 to 5 minutes, or until the cheese is golden. **Remove the bay leaves** and ladle the soup into bowls. Top each with a slice of toasted cheese bread and serve.

Broccoli Cheese Soup

One of the first things you learn in the restaurant business is never to let a cream soup come to a boil, 'cause it will "break," or separate. A gentle simmer is all it needs.

8 TO 10 SERVINGS

½ cup (1 stick) butter, softened
½ cup all-purpose flour
3 cans (14½ ounces each)
   ready-to-use chicken broth
2 bunches broccoli, trimmed
   and chopped
1 small onion, diced
1 teaspoon black pepper
1 cup (½ pint) heavy cream
3 cups (12 ounces) shredded
   Cheddar cheese

TIPS FROM THE PROS

Serve the soup in edible bread bowls that you make by cutting a circle out of the tops of kaiser rolls and hollowing them out. Ladle the soup into the bread bowls and garnish with additional shredded Cheddar cheese. It's so easy to make this into a real "wow!"

In a small bowl, combine the butter and flour and blend until smooth; set aside. In a soup pot, combine the broth, broccoli, onion, and pepper and bring to a boil over high heat. Reduce the heat to low, cover, and simmer for 25 to 30 minutes, or until the broccoli is very tender. Stir in the butter mixture until the soup is thickened. Slowly stir in the heavy cream, mixing well. Add the cheese 1 cup at a time, mixing well after each addition, until the cheese is melted.

Hot-and-Sour Soup

At Chinese restaurants, it seems that every meal starts with a steaming bowl of soup. Many people prefer wonton, others prefer egg drop. My personal favorite is hot-and-sour soup and, after a number of attempts to duplicate the restaurant taste at home, I think I came pretty close. Try it and see if you agree.

4 TO 5 SERVINGS

2 cans (14½ ounces each) ready-to-use chicken broth, divided
2 tablespoons cornstarch
½ pound firm tofu, cut into small chunks
¼ pound sliced fresh
  mushrooms
3 tablespoons soy sauce
3 tablespoons white vinegar
1 teaspoon ground ginger
1 teaspoon black pepper
1 egg, lightly beaten
1 cup fresh bean sprouts
½ teaspoon sesame oil

TIPS FROM THE PROS

Top each bowl with thinly sliced scallions and serve with Chinese noodles.

In a small bowl, combine ¼ cup chicken broth and the cornstarch; mix well and set aside. In a soup pot, combine the remaining chicken broth, the tofu, mushrooms, soy sauce, vinegar, ginger, and pepper; mix well and bring to a boil over high heat. Reduce the heat to low; stir in the cornstarch mixture until thickened. Slowly stir in the beaten egg to form egg strands. Add the bean sprouts and simmer for 1 to 2 minutes, or until heated through, stirring occasionally. Add the sesame oil; mix well and serve.

Potato-Cheese Soup

Have you ever wondered why potato-cheese soup is often the soup of the day in restaurants? It's because it allows the chefs to use up leftover mashed or baked potatoes and assorted pieces of cheese. Our version starts with raw potatoes, since most of us don't regularly have extra cooked spuds hanging around our kitchens!

4 TO 6 SERVINGS

2 tablespoons butter
1 rib celery, finely diced
1 small onion, finely diced
1 can (14½ ounces)
   ready-to-use chicken broth
3 large potatoes, peeled and
   diced
2 teaspoons white vinegar
3 tablespoons all-purpose flour
2½ cups milk
¼ teaspoon salt
1 teaspoon black pepper
2 cups (8 ounces) shredded Cheddar cheese

TIPS FROM THE PROS

To serve this restaurant-style, top with bacon bits, sliced scallions, and additional shredded cheese.

In a soup pot, melt the butter over medium-high heat. Add the celery and onion and sauté for 5 to 7 minutes, or until tender. Add the chicken broth, potatoes, and vinegar; cover and bring to a boil. Reduce the heat to low and simmer for 20 to 25 minutes, or until the potatoes are tender. Add the flour, milk, salt, and pepper; cook until the soup is thickened and heated through, stirring constantly. Add the cheese and stir until melted. Serve immediately.

Manhattan Clam Chowder

People are always asking me the difference between Manhattan and New England clam chowder. It's the tomatoes that make this version different from the creamy white New England style. After you try this and my recipe for New England-style clam chowder (opposite page), let me know which type is your favorite.

6 TO 8 SERVINGS

4 slices bacon, minced
2 ribs celery, chopped
2 medium carrots, chopped
1 large onion, chopped
3 medium potatoes, peeled and diced
2 cans (14½ ounces each) diced tomatoes, undrained
2 cans (10 ounces each) baby clams, undrained
2 bottles (8 ounces each) clam juice
1 teaspoon dried thyme

TIPS FROM THE PROS

Freezing the bacon makes it easy to mince. If it's not frozen, try mincing it with kitchen shears.

In a soup pot, cook the bacon for 3 to 5 minutes over high heat, until crisp. Add the celery, carrots, and onion and sauté for 5 to 7 minutes, or until the onion is tender, stirring frequently. Add the remaining ingredients, cover, and bring to a boil. Reduce the heat to low and simmer, covered, for 55 to 65 minutes, or until the potatoes are very tender.

New England Clam Chowder

Let's take a trip to a small seaside shack in New England for some tasty cream-style clam chowder. Well, when we can't, a bowl of this one topped with crispy oyster crackers is the next best thing!

4 TO 6 SERVINGS

1 small onion, chopped
2 ounces salt pork, diced
2 cans (6½ ounces each) chopped clams, undrained
1 bottle (8 ounces) clam juice
1 can (14½ ounces) ready-to-use chicken broth
1 large potato, peeled and diced
¼ teaspoon salt
¼ teaspoon black pepper
3 tablespoons cornstarch
2 cups (1 pint) heavy cream, divided
¼ cup chopped fresh parsley

In a soup pot, sauté the onion and salt pork over medium heat for 3 to 5 minutes, until the onion is tender. Add the clams, clam juice, chicken broth, potato, salt, and pepper; cover and bring to a boil. Cook, covered, for 12 to 15 minutes, until the potatoes are tender. In a small bowl, dissolve the cornstarch in ½ cup cream; add to the soup. Add the remaining 1½ cups cream and the parsley; cook for 5 minutes, or until thickened, stirring frequently.

Vegetable Beef Barley Soup

There's nothing like the aroma of a homemade soup that's been simmering on the stove all day. Restaurants can afford to take that much time to make their soups, but most of us can't! Well, we can still enjoy the same taste and smell of this hearty soup in our kitchens . . . and in no time!

10 TO 12 SERVINGS

7 cups water
3 cans (10½ ounces each) condensed beef broth
1 pound beef stew meat, cut into ½-inch chunks
2 large onions, chopped
1 pound sliced fresh mushrooms
4 medium carrots, sliced
1 can (14½ ounces) diced tomatoes, drained
½ teaspoon salt
¾ teaspoon black pepper
1 cup quick-cooking pearl barley

In a soup pot, combine all the ingredients except the barley; cover and bring to a boil over high heat. Reduce the heat to low and simmer, covered, for 20 minutes, stirring occasionally. Add the barley and simmer for 15 to 20 minutes more, or until the barley is tender.

Wedding Soup

I've only seen this soup on a few restaurant menus and, when I have, I've always ordered it. If you've never been fortunate enough to try it, I suggest you add my easy version to your "weeknight serve it up in the kitchen" menu.

6 TO 8 SERVINGS

½ pound ground beef
¼ cup Italian-flavored bread crumbs
4¼ cups water, divided
¾ teaspoon black pepper, divided
3 cans (10½ ounces each) condensed chicken broth
½ cup chopped fresh spinach
2 medium carrots, finely chopped
½ cup uncooked tiny shell pasta
¼ cup grated Parmesan cheese

In a medium bowl, combine the ground beef, bread crumbs, ¼ cup water, and ¼ teaspoon pepper; mix well and form into ½-inch meatballs. In a soup pot, combine the chicken broth, spinach, carrots, the meatballs, and the remaining 4 cups water and ½ teaspoon pepper. Cover and bring to a boil over high heat. Reduce the heat to low and simmer, covered, for 30 minutes. Add the pasta, increase the heat to medium, and cook for 8 to 10 minutes, or until the pasta is tender. Sprinkle with the Parmesan cheese and serve.

Hearty Minestrone

Traditional restaurant-style minestrone soup is slow-cooked for hours and hours before it's served as an appetizer or even as a main course. My easy version is ready in no time, but each bowlful is overflowing with that slow-cooked flavor.

10 TO 12 SERVINGS

3 cans (14½ ounces each) ready-to-use beef broth

1 can (15 ounces) red kidney
   beans, undrained

1 can (16 to 20 ounces)
   cannellini beans, undrained

1 jar (26 ounces) spaghetti
   sauce

1 package (10 ounces) frozen
   chopped spinach, thawed

1 package (10 ounces) frozen
   mixed vegetables, thawed

1 small onion, chopped

1 teaspoon garlic powder

½ teaspoon black pepper

1 cup uncooked elbow macaroni

TIPS FROM THE PROS

For added flavor, top each bowl with a little grated Romano or Parmesan cheese. Of course, fresh-grated cheese is the way to go when you've got it!

In a soup pot, combine all the ingredients except the macaroni. Bring to a boil over high heat, stirring occasionally. Stir in the macaroni. Reduce the heat to low and simmer for 30 minutes, stirring occasionally.

Pasta e Fagiole

Translated from the Italian, the name of this soup is pasta and beans. My version's pretty simple to make, yet after just one spoonful you'll be sure to agree that there's nothing simple-tasting about this soup!

8 TO 10 SERVINGS

2 tablespoons olive oil
2 medium onions, chopped
6 garlic cloves, minced
3 cans (14½ ounces each)
   ready-to-use chicken broth
2 cans (16 to 20 ounces each)
   cannellini beans, undrained
1 can (14½ ounces) diced
   tomatoes, undrained
½ teaspoon salt
1 teaspoon black pepper
1 cup uncooked ditalini or
   other small pasta shape
½ cup chopped fresh parsley

TIPS FROM THE PROS

Give this a finishing touch
(for both looks and taste!)
by topping each serving with a
bit of fresh-grated Parmesan cheese.

In a large soup pot, heat the oil over medium heat; sauté the onions and garlic for about 10 minutes, or until the onions are tender. Stir in the chicken broth, 1 can of the cannellini beans, the tomatoes, salt, and pepper; cook for 30 minutes, stirring occasionally. Meanwhile, cook the pasta according to the package directions; drain. Using a potato masher, gently mash the beans and tomatoes in the soup pot. Add the remaining can of beans, the parsley, and the cooked pasta. Reduce the heat to low and simmer for 30 minutes, stirring occasionally.

Black Bean Soup

On a cool fall day, you can hang a sign outside your kitchen that says, "Today's Special: Black Bean Soup." And when your family comes running to the table, they're gonna need big bowls, 'cause a cup of this soup is never enough!

8 TO 10 SERVINGS

2 cans (10½ ounces each)
   condensed chicken broth
3 cups water
1 medium onion, chopped
4 cans (15 ounces each) black
   beans, undrained
1 jar (16 ounces) salsa
½ teaspoon ground cumin

TIPS FROM THE PROS

Garnish each bowl with a dollop of sour cream or some shredded Monterey Jack cheese and jalapeño pepper slices.

In a soup pot, combine the broth, water, and onion over medium heat. Cook for 5 minutes, or until the onion is tender, then reduce the heat to medium-low. In a blender, purée 2 cans of the black beans with their liquid until smooth. Add to the soup pot along with the remaining undrained beans. Stir in the salsa and cumin and simmer for 10 minutes, or until thoroughly heated, stirring occasionally.

Chicken Noodle Soup

Not only do those New York City delis make darned good sandwiches, but their soups are known to be pretty incredible, too, especially the homemade chicken soup. And when we prepare it the same way they do, boy, are we in for a real treat.

6 TO 8 SERVINGS

One 3- to 3½-pound chicken,
   cut into 8 pieces
3 carrots, cut into 1-inch
   pieces
3 ribs celery, cut into 1-inch
   pieces
1 medium onion, quartered
8 cups water
2½ teaspoons salt
½ teaspoon black pepper
2 cups cooked egg noodles

HELPFUL HINTS

For chicken rice soup, add 2 cups cooked rice in place of the noodles.

In a soup pot, combine all the ingredients except the noodles and bring to a boil over high heat. Reduce the heat to medium-low, cover, and simmer for 2½ to 3 hours, or until the chicken easily falls off the bones. Remove the chicken from the pot. Allow the chicken to cool slightly, then remove and discard the skin and bones and cut the meat into bite-sized pieces. Return the chicken to the pot, add the noodles, and cook over medium heat until heated through.

Wonton Soup

When you order wonton soup in a restaurant, do you always wish there were more wontons in your bowl? Problem solved! Make this easy version of wonton soup at home and add lots of extra wontons to every bowl. It's the same awesome restaurant taste, with plenty of wontons.

5 TO 7 SERVINGS

¼ pound ground pork
3 scallions, thinly sliced, divided
¼ teaspoon ground ginger
⅛ teaspoon garlic powder
1 package (6 ounces) wonton skins
1 egg, beaten
3 cans (14½ ounces each) ready-to-use chicken broth
1½ cups water
1 tablespoon soy sauce
¼ pound sliced fresh mushrooms

TIPS FROM THE PROS

Restaurants generally cook wontons in boiling water, then add them to soup just before serving. Here we've simplified things by cooking them right in the soup. Oh—you can also make wontons using other ingredients like shrimp and water chestnuts in the filling.

In a medium bowl, combine the ground pork, one third of the sliced scallions, the ginger, and garlic powder; mix well. Place the wonton skins on a work surface, then place a teaspoonful of the pork mixture in the center of each. Brush the egg around the edges of the wonton skin, bring 2 opposing corners up to meet and press to seal. Moisten the remaining corners and fold each one up to meet the other corner; press to seal. Meanwhile, in a soup pot, combine the chicken broth, water, soy sauce, and mushrooms and bring to a boil over medium-high heat. Carefully drop the wontons into the soup along with the remaining sliced scallions and cook for 8 to 10 minutes, or until the wontons are tender.

SALADS AND SUCH

Caesar Salad

When it comes to making Caesar salad, every restaurant seems to have its own style. I like the light style and I like the creamy style, so I created this version that's truly the best of both worlds.

4 TO 6 SERVINGS

1 head romaine lettuce, cut
   into bite-sized pieces
2 cups croutons
1 cup mayonnaise
½ cup milk
2 tablespoons fresh lemon
   juice
½ cup plus 1 tablespoon grated
   Parmesan cheese, divided
2 garlic cloves, minced
½ teaspoon salt
½ teaspoon black pepper
1 can (2 ounces) anchovies in oil, drained

TIPS FROM THE PROS

This can be turned into a chicken Caesar salad meal by arranging the salad on plates and topping with strips of grilled boneless, skinless chicken breasts.

In a large salad bowl, combine the romaine and croutons; set aside. In a medium bowl, combine the mayonnaise, milk, lemon juice, ½ cup Parmesan cheese, the garlic, salt, and pepper; whisk until smooth and creamy. Add the dressing to the lettuce and croutons; toss to coat well. Top with the anchovies and sprinkle with the remaining 1 tablespoon Parmesan cheese. Serve immediately.

Cobb Salad

These days, Cobb salad is a standard menu item at restaurants from coast to coast, but did you know that it started as a way to use leftovers at the Brown Derby restaurant in California?

4 TO 6 SERVINGS

4 boneless, skinless chicken breast halves,
  (1 to 1¼ pounds total), pounded to a ¼-inch thickness
½ teaspoon salt
¼ teaspoon black pepper
1 medium head iceberg
  lettuce, cut bite-sized
4 slices crumbled cooked
  bacon
3 hard-boiled eggs, coarsely
  chopped
1 avocado, pitted, peeled, and
  coarsely chopped
1 large tomato, coarsely
  chopped
1 can (2¼ ounces) sliced black olives, drained
¼ pound blue cheese, cut into ½-inch chunks

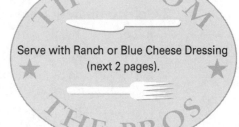

TIPS FROM THE PROS

Serve with Ranch or Blue Cheese Dressing (next 2 pages).

Season the chicken with salt and pepper. Coat a large skillet with non-stick cooking spray; cook the chicken over medium-high heat for 3 to 4 minutes per side, until no pink remains. Remove the chicken; set aside to cool slightly, then cut into ½-inch chunks. Meanwhile, cover a large platter with lettuce. Place the cooked chicken in a row in the center. Place the bacon in a row on one side of the chicken, then a row of eggs, then avocado. On the other side of the chicken, place a row of tomato, then a row of olives, then blue cheese chunks. Serve immediately.

Ranch Dressing

At one time or another we've all fallen into the bottled salad dressing rut and wished for a fresh flavor to drizzle on our greens or toss with our tomatoes. Why not make your own dressings? I always do! They're easy, tasty, and inexpensive, too!

ABOUT 1 CUP

1 cup mayonnaise
¼ cup buttermilk
1 teaspoon white vinegar
1 garlic clove, minced
1 teaspoon minced fresh dill
⅛ teaspoon sugar

In a medium bowl, combine all the ingredients; whisk until smooth. Serve, or cover and chill until ready to serve.

Blue Cheese Dressing

This is one of my all-time favorites!

ABOUT 1 CUP

¾ cup sour cream
¼ cup mayonnaise
1 teaspoon vegetable oil
1½ teaspoons white vinegar
⅛ teaspoon sugar
⅛ teaspoon salt
⅛ teaspoon black pepper
1 package (4 ounces) crumbled blue cheese

In a medium bowl, combine all the ingredients except the blue cheese; whisk until smooth. Add the blue cheese and stir until well combined. Serve, or cover and chill until ready to serve.

Spinach Salad with Hot Bacon Dressing

If you've ever tried hot bacon dressing on a cool crisp salad, I bet you haven't been able to forget that tasty combination. The first time I tried this salad was in a small Rhode Island café, and it's still one of my favorites. Now I'm gonna share this chef's special with you.

4 TO 6 SERVINGS

8 slices bacon, chopped
¼ cup apple cider vinegar
2 teaspoons fresh lemon juice
2 tablespoons sugar
¼ teaspoon black pepper
1 package (10 ounces) fresh
   spinach, washed and
   trimmed
1 hard-boiled egg, chopped

TIPS FROM THE PROS

You can prepare the spinach and dressing in advance; then, when you're ready to eat, heat the dressing, toss, top, and serve.

In a large skillet, cook the bacon over medium-high heat until crisp. Add the vinegar, lemon juice, sugar, and pepper; mix well. Place the spinach in a serving bowl; add the hot bacon dressing and toss to coat. Sprinkle with the egg and serve immediately.

Taco Salad

Olé! Take a bite of this colorful salad and you're think you're in a Mexican restaurant. To make it even more authentic, serve it in a crunchy tortilla bowl.

4 SERVINGS

1 pound ground beef
1 envelope (1¼ ounces) taco
  seasoning mix
4 Tortilla Bowls (opposite page)
1 small head iceberg lettuce,
  chopped
1 can (15 ounces) red kidney
  beans, rinsed and drained
1 large tomato, diced
1 cup (4 ounces) shredded
  Cheddar cheese
1 can (2¼ ounces) sliced black
  olives, drained
½ cup sour cream
¾ cup salsa

HELPFUL HINT

If you'd rather serve this without making tortilla bowls, just layer the salad in individual bowls or a large glass serving bowl.

HELPFUL HINTS

In a medium skillet, brown the ground beef with the taco seasoning mix over medium-high heat, stirring to break up the meat; drain and allow to cool slightly. In the tortilla bowls, layer the lettuce, beans, ground beef mixture, tomato, cheese, and olives. Dollop with the sour cream and salsa and serve.

Tortilla Bowls

Fill these edible South-of-the-Border-style bowls with your favorite taco salad or any other garden salad favorite.

---

4 EDIBLE BOWLS

Four 10-inch flour tortillas, at room temperature
Nonstick cooking spray

Preheat the oven to 425°F. Place 4 ovenproof soup bowls on a rimmed baking sheet. Coat both sides of each tortilla with nonstick cooking spray. Carefully mold the tortillas into the bowls. Stack another oven-proof bowl in each tortilla. (If you don't have eight ovenproof bowls, bake these one or two at a time.) Bake for 7 to 9 minutes, or until the tortillas hold their shape. Carefully remove the top bowls and bake the tortillas (still in the bottom bowls) for 3 to 4 more minutes, or until the tortillas are golden and crisp. Remove the tortillas from the bowls and allow to cool on a wire rack. Fill with your favorite salad and serve immediately.

Greek Island Salad

I'll admit it—I didn't get this recipe from a restaurant, but from a Greek Festival. Oh, the music, the dancing, and, of course, this salad! It was a truly unforgettable event.

4 TO 6 SERVINGS

¾ cup olive oil
Juice of 2 lemons
1 tablespoon dried oregano
½ teaspoon garlic powder
½ teaspoon salt
¼ teaspoon black pepper
1 medium head iceberg
    lettuce, cut into 1-inch
    chunks
1 medium cucumber, peeled
    and diced
1 package (4 ounces)
    crumbled feta cheese
2 medium tomatoes, cut into wedges
1 can (6 ounces) pitted large black olives or Greek olives,
    drained

HELPFUL HINTS

Greek olives can be found at most supermarket deli counters or in the ethnic foods section.

In a small bowl, combine the olive oil, lemon juice, oregano, garlic powder, salt, and pepper; mix well. Place the chopped lettuce on a platter. Top with the cucumber, then sprinkle with the feta cheese. Arrange the tomatoes over the cheese, then top the salad with the olives. Drizzle the dressing over the salad and serve.

Tabbouleh Salad

Ever get a craving for a salad that's a little different? You know, an exotic-tasting dish that you can actually make at home? Go ahead and try this tabbouleh salad. It's just like the ones found on Middle Eastern menus.

6 TO 8 SERVINGS

1 cup bulgur wheat

2 cups hot water

1 tablespoon olive or
vegetable oil

⅓ cup fresh lemon juice

1 teaspoon minced garlic

2 tablespoons minced fresh
mint

1 teaspoon salt

¼ teaspoon black pepper

1 medium tomato, finely
chopped

½ small cucumber, finely chopped

6 scallions, thinly sliced

2 cups coarsely chopped fresh parsley

TIPS FROM THE PROS

A shortcut for chopping the parsley—without really chopping—is to use kitchen shears and simply snip the leaves off the stems in small pieces. Oh, pita wedges are great for serving along with this salad.

In a large bowl, combine the bulgur wheat and hot water and allow to stand for 20 to 30 minutes, or until the water is completely absorbed. Add the oil, lemon juice, garlic, mint, salt, and pepper; mix until thoroughly combined. Add the remaining ingredients and toss until well combined. Cover and chill for at least 1 hour before serving.

Fresh Mozzarella and Tomato Salad

If you're a tomato and cheese lover like me, then I suggest you plan on adding this salad to your weekly menu. The combination of juicy ripe tomato and creamy mild cheese is irresistible!

4 TO 6 SERVINGS

2 large ripe tomatoes, cut into
¼-inch slices
½ pound fresh mozzarella, cut
into ¼-inch slices
¼ cup olive oil
2 tablespoons balsamic
vinegar
1 tablespoon chopped fresh
basil
½ teaspoon salt
½ teaspoon coarse-ground
black pepper

TIPS FROM THE PROS

This is easy to make ahead of time; just cover and chill the platter and dressing separately. When you're ready to serve, drizzle the tomatoes and mozzarella with the dressing and, if desired, garnish your platter with sprigs of basil.

Alternate the tomato and mozzarella slices on a serving platter. In a small bowl, combine the remaining ingredients; mix well. Drizzle over the tomato and cheese slices and serve.

Country Club Fruit Salad

Turn your kitchen into the private dining room of a country club when you serve up this fruit salad dressed in its light, lively yogurt sauce.

---

4 SERVINGS

---

1 container (8 ounces) low-fat
　　vanilla yogurt
½ cup honey
Juice of ½ orange
¼ teaspoon grated orange peel
¼ teaspoon salt
1 cantaloupe, peeled and cut
　　into chunks
½ honeydew melon, peeled
　　and cut into chunks
2 oranges, peeled and sliced
2 kiwis, peeled and sliced
1 pint fresh strawberries, washed and hulled

TIPS FROM THE PROS

To make a deluxe fruit platter, add a scoop of cottage cheese or fruit sorbet to each serving. You can also add any other favorite fruit.

In a medium bowl, combine the yogurt, honey, orange juice, orange peel, and salt; mix well. Arrange an assortment of the fruit on each of four individual plates and drizzle with the yogurt dressing. Serve immediately.

Tarragon Chicken Salad

Why make ordinary chicken salad when you can prepare the one that's a favorite at trendy bistros and delis throughout the country? All it takes is a few extra spices and you've got a chicken salad that's worth talking about.

4 TO 6 SERVINGS

1 can (14½ ounces) ready-to-use chicken broth
⅛ teaspoon black pepper
1½ pounds boneless, skinless
    chicken breasts
1 cup mayonnaise
1 tablespoon apple cider
    vinegar
1 scallion, thinly sliced
¼ cup chopped fresh parsley
2 tablespoons chopped fresh
    tarragon
⅛ teaspoon ground red pepper
⅛ teaspoon sugar

TIPS FROM THE PROS

A fancy way to serve this is to place a scoop of chicken salad on a romaine lettuce leaf and surround it with slices of fresh melon. The salad is also nice served in a split croissant.

In a medium saucepan, combine the chicken broth and black pepper and bring to a boil over high heat. Add the chicken and cook for 10 to 15 minutes, or until no pink remains. Meanwhile, in a medium bowl, combine the remaining ingredients; mix well. Remove the chicken from the broth; allow to cool slightly, then cut into ½-inch pieces. Add the chicken to the mayonnaise mixture; mix well. Cover and chill for at least 2 hours before serving.

Classy French Dip

What's in a name? A lot when it comes to this all-time favorite sandwich, because it's simply thinly sliced roast beef served in a roll with a bit of broth for dunking. Sure, it tastes great, but once we call it a French dip . . . it's so much more exciting!

6 SANDWICHES

1 can (14½ ounces) ready-to-use beef broth
½ teaspoon black pepper
½ teaspoon garlic powder
½ teaspoon onion powder
2 pounds thinly sliced deli roast beef
6 French bread rolls, split

In a large skillet, combine the broth, pepper, garlic powder, and onion powder. Bring to a boil over medium heat, then stir in the roast beef. Cook for 3 to 4 minutes, or until the beef is heated through. Use tongs to arrange the beef evenly over the open rolls and serve with individual bowls of the broth mixture for dipping.

Grilled Chicken Sandwiches

We're seeing more and more grilled chicken sandwiches at all styles of restaurants, from fast food to fancy ones with four-star ratings. And no matter what kind of restaurant we're eating at, our chicken sandwich is bound to be flavored with a savory sauce, just like these are.

4 SANDWICHES

4 boneless, skinless, chicken breast halves (1 to 1¼ pounds total), pounded to a ¼-inch thickness
1 package (0.7 ounce) dry Italian salad dressing mix
½ cup mayonnaise
2 teaspoons fresh lemon juice
1 teaspoon garlic powder
4 kaiser rolls, split
¼ head iceberg lettuce, shredded
1 large tomato, sliced

In a medium bowl, combine the chicken and salad dressing mix, tossing to coat the chicken completely; cover and marinate in the refrigerator for 30 minutes. Preheat a grill pan over medium-high heat and grill the chicken for 3 to 4 minutes per side, or until no pink remains. Meanwhile, in a medium bowl, combine the mayonnaise, lemon juice, and garlic powder; mix well. Spread over the cut sides of the rolls. Top the bottom halves of the rolls with the lettuce, chicken, and tomato. Replace the tops of the rolls and serve.

Thanksgiving Dinner Sandwiches

Does this sound crazy to you? It did to me the first time I ordered it at a restaurant in Syracuse, New York. The waitress insisted it was one of the most popular combos on the menu. After I finished every last bite, I knew why!

4 SANDWICHES

1 pound sliced deli turkey breast
2 cups hot prepared stuffing
1 cup whole-berry cranberry sauce
Four 6-inch hoagie rolls, split

Preheat the oven to 350°F. Place an equal amount of the turkey, stuffing, and cranberry sauce in each hoagie roll. Wrap each sandwich in a piece of aluminum foil and bake for 15 to 20 minutes, or until heated through. Carefully unwrap and serve.

Open-Faced Reuben Sandwiches

Some of the biggest and best delis serve their Reubens open-faced, just like this recipe that I got from a deli in central New York. It's one of the best Reubens I've ever tasted.

4 SERVINGS

½ cup mayonnaise

2 tablespoons ketchup

2 tablespoons sweet pickle relish

⅛ teaspoon garlic powder

⅛ teaspoon salt

⅛ teaspoon black pepper

8 slices rye bread

1 pound sliced deli corned beef

2 cans (14½ ounces each) sauerkraut, rinsed and well drained

8 slices (6 ounces) Swiss cheese

TIPS FROM THE PROS

You might want to use only half of the dressing on the sandwiches before baking, then top each with a dollop of the remaining dressing before serving.

Preheat the oven to 450°F. In a medium bowl, combine the mayonnaise, ketchup, relish, garlic powder, salt, and pepper; mix well. Arrange the bread on two baking sheets. Spread some dressing mixture on each slice (see Tips from the Pros). Top each with corned beef, sauerkraut, and a slice of Swiss cheese. Bake for 6 to 8 minutes, or until heated through and the cheese is melted. Place 2 topped bread slices on each plate and serve.

Quick-and-Easy Gyros

Did you know that the name "gyro" comes from the Greek word gyros, *meaning a "turn"? It refers to the fact that gyros are made from rotisserie-roasted seasoned lamb that turns constantly as it cooks. Look how easy it is to re-create that same fancy taste without lots of fancy equipment or long cooking.*

6 GYROS

1 cup sour cream
1 large cucumber, halved, seeded and chopped
1 teaspoon garlic powder, divided
1¼ teaspoons salt, divided
½ teaspoon black pepper, divided
1 pound ground lamb
½ small onion, finely chopped
¼ cup finely chopped fresh parsley
Six 6-inch pita breads, cut in half
¾ cup shredded lettuce
1 medium tomato, diced

Preheat the oven to 350°F. In a food processor, combine the sour cream, cucumber, ½ teaspoon garlic powder, and ¼ teaspoon each of the salt and pepper; process until the desired consistency for a sauce. Cover and chill for 1 hour. Meanwhile, in a medium bowl, combine the lamb, onion, parsley, and the remaining ½ teaspoon garlic powder, 1 teaspoon salt, and ¼ teaspoon pepper; mix well and press into a 9" × 5" loaf pan. Bake for 40 to 45 minutes, or until the juices run clear and no pink remains. Allow to cool for 5 to 10 minutes, then thinly slice the meat loaf and place in the pita halves. Top with the lettuce, tomato, and cucumber sauce. Serve immediately.

Baked Italian Hoagies

You don't need a restaurant-style brick oven to make sub shop–style crusty baked subs. Simply prepare your sandwich, wrap it snugly in foil, pop it in the oven, and wait. Once you unwrap this hearty delight, I'm sure you'll agree—it's a real showstopper.

6 HOAGIES

Six 6- to 8-inch hoagie rolls, split
½ cup Italian dressing
½ pound sliced deli salami
½ pound sliced deli turkey
½ pound sliced deli ham
½ pound sliced deli provolone cheese
1 large tomato, thinly sliced
½ medium onion, thinly sliced

Preheat the oven to 375°F. Brush the cut sides of the rolls with the Italian dressing. Layer the bottom halves with the salami, turkey, ham, cheese, tomato, and onion and replace the tops. Place each on a piece of aluminum foil and wrap tightly. Bake for 12 to 15 minutes, or until the cheese is melted. Carefully remove the aluminum foil and serve.

Piled-High Club Sandwiches

Have you ever gone into a restaurant and been handed a huge menu that had so many things on it you liked that you just couldn't decide what to order? I wouldn't be surprised if your eyes searched the menu until they settled on that old standby, the piled-high club sandwich. It's usually served up with a mound of thick-cut French fries, and, if it's made like this one, you're guaranteed to be pleased!

4 OVERSIZED SANDWICHES

12 slices white bread, toasted
½ cup mayonnaise
¼ head iceberg lettuce,
    leaves separated
½ pound sliced deli turkey
1 large tomato, cut into
    8 slices
8 slices bacon, cooked until
    crisp

16 sandwich toothpicks

TIPS FROM THE PROS

Any bread variety will work, including whole wheat and sourdough, but for the best-looking sandwich wedges, make sure to start with square bread slices.

Spread one side of each piece of toast with mayonnaise. Place 4 slices mayonnaise side up on a cutting board. Top each with a quarter of the lettuce and turkey, a second piece of toast, 2 tomato slices, 2 slices bacon, and another piece of toast, mayonnaise side down. Secure each with 4 toothpicks, then slice each sandwich with two diagonal cuts, from corner to corner, into quarters. Arrange each sandwich on a plate, with the points of the sandwiches facing out, and serve.

Pulled Pork Sandwiches

In the South, it seems like there's a barbecue joint on every corner and each one boasts the best pulled pork sandwiches. The Southern cooks in my test kitchen helped me create a version that comes pretty close to that authentic flavor, but with a shortcut or two. Y'all will see!

8 SANDWICHES

One 3- to 3½-pound boneless
    pork shoulder blade roast
1 teaspoon salt
1 teaspoon black pepper
2 tablespoons vegetable oil
2¾ cups water
2 tablespoons white vinegar
¼ cup sugar
½ teaspoon liquid smoke
8 hamburger buns, split
1½ cups warm barbecue sauce
    (see Helpful Hints)

HELPFUL HINTS

Use your favorite barbecue sauce or make one of the recipes on the following pages.

Season the roast with the salt and pepper. Heat the oil in a 6-quart pressure cooker over high heat. Add the roast and brown on all sides, 8 to 10 minutes. Add the water, vinegar, sugar, and liquid smoke. Lock the lid in place and bring to full pressure over high heat. When the pressure regulator begins to rock, reduce the heat to medium and cook for 1 hour. Cool the cooker at once by carefully placing under cold running water until steam no longer escapes from the vent and the pressure is completely reduced. Remove the lid, remove the roast from the pot, and cut into 1-inch-thick slices (the roast will come apart as you slice). Divide the meat equally over the hamburger buns. Top with the barbecue sauce and serve.

Sweet Barbecue Sauce

Why not try this or one of the next 2 homemade barbecue sauces with your pulled pork sandwiches? Each one hails from a different part of the South since each area has its own specialty sauce. I guarantee that you'll never go back to the bottled stuff again.

ABOUT 1½ CUPS

1 cup ketchup
¼ cup lemon juice
¼ cup (½ stick) butter
¼ cup packed dark brown sugar
1 small onion, finely chopped
1 garlic clove, minced
2 tablespoons yellow mustard
2 tablespoons Worcestershire sauce

In a large saucepan, combine all the ingredients over medium heat. Bring to a boil and allow to boil for 15 minutes, or until the sauce is thick and the onion is tender, stirring frequently. Serve warm.

Lip-Smackin' Barbecue Sauce

The name says it all . . . except that this cider vinegar-based sauce is popular throughout the Carolinas and Alabama.

ABOUT 1½ CUPS

1 cup apple cider vinegar
1 cup ketchup
¼ cup water
2 teaspoons yellow mustard
1 teaspoon Worcestershire sauce
1 teaspoon chili powder
¼ teaspoon ground red pepper
½ teaspoon salt
2 teaspoons black pepper

In a large saucepan, combine all the ingredients over medium heat. Bring to a boil and allow to boil for 15 to 20 minutes, or until slightly thickened, stirring frequently. Serve warm.

North Carolina Barbecue Sauce

This tongue-tingling sauce gets its kick from more than half of its zippy ingredients. Wow!

ABOUT 1½ CUPS

1 cup apple cider vinegar
⅔ cup yellow mustard
½ cup packed light brown sugar
2 tablespoons butter
1 teaspoon soy sauce
1 teaspoon chili powder
¼ teaspoon ground red pepper
1 teaspoon black pepper

In a large saucepan, combine all the ingredients over medium heat. Bring to a boil and allow to boil for 5 minutes, or until the sauce is thickened, stirring constantly. Serve warm.

Italian Meatball Subs

Some good friends of mine who own an Italian restaurant in Upstate New York shared a tip with me years ago that I use over and over. The next time you make meatballs, instead of using dry bread crumbs, try using cut-up slices of white bread. It makes your meatballs come out moister and tastier every time!

4 SANDWICHES

1 jar (26 ounces) spaghetti
    sauce, divided
1 pound ground beef
2 slices white bread, cut up
    into small pieces
1 small onion, finely chopped
¼ cup grated Parmesan cheese
1 egg
1 teaspoon dried parsley
1 teaspoon garlic powder
Four 6-inch hoagie rolls, split

TIPS FROM THE PROS

For a real finished look, grate fresh Parmesan cheese over the meatballs just before serving.

In a large bowl, combine ⅓ cup spaghetti sauce, the ground beef, bread, onion, Parmesan cheese, egg, parsley, and garlic powder; mix well. Shape into sixteen 2-inch meatballs. Meanwhile, in a soup pot, bring the remaining spaghetti sauce to a boil over medium heat. Reduce the heat to medium-low. Add the meatballs, cover, and simmer for about 30 minutes. Place the meatballs in the rolls, top with sauce, and serve.

Philadelphia Cheese Steak Sandwiches

There's a little joint in Philly where I go whenever I travel to the QVC studios in nearby West Chester, PA. They make the best cheese steak sandwiches, so I begged them to share their secret recipe. When you see how they do it, you won't believe how easy it is.

4 SANDWICHES

3 tablespoons vegetable oil
2 large green bell peppers, cut
   into ¼-inch strips
2 large onions, thinly sliced
1¼ pounds beef top round,
   thinly sliced (see Helpful
   Hints)
½ teaspoon black pepper
4 hoagie rolls, split
1 cup Cheese Whiz, melted

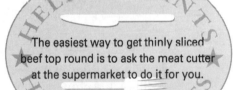

HELPFUL HINTS

The easiest way to get thinly sliced beef top round is to ask the meat cutter at the supermarket to do it for you.

Heat the oil in a large skillet over medium-high heat. Add the bell peppers and sauté for 10 minutes. Add the onions and sauté for 5 to 7 minutes, or until the onions are tender. Transfer to a medium bowl, cover, and set aside. Add the beef to the skillet and sprinkle with the black pepper; sauté for 3 to 5 minutes, or until no pink remains in the beef. Return the peppers and onions to the skillet and cook for 2 to 3 minutes, or until heated through. Place the mixture over the hoagie rolls, drizzle with the melted cheese, and serve immediately.

Mr. Food's Fast Burgers

When you want that taste of fast-food burgers without going out, you can make them at home in no time! And since all the fast-food burger places are now making our burgers just the way we want them, you should feel free to do the same by substituting your favorite toppings for any of mine.

4 HAMBURGERS

4 large uncut sesame seed rolls
1 pound ground beef
1 tablespoon butter
½ cup Thousand Island dressing
2 cups shredded lettuce
4 slices (4 ounces) American cheese
1 small onion, finely chopped
8 dill pickle chips

Cut each roll horizontally into 3 sections; set aside. Form the ground beef into 8 thin patties. Melt the butter in a large skillet over medium-low heat and cook the patties in batches for 3 to 4 minutes per side, or until no longer pink. Spread half of the dressing over the four bottom roll sections, then sprinkle with half of the lettuce. Place a hamburger patty on each and top with a slice of cheese. Sprinkle the onion over the cheese, then top with the center roll sections. Spread the remaining dressing over the top of the center roll sections, then sprinkle with the remaining lettuce. Top each with another hamburger patty, 2 dill pickles, and the top roll section. Serve, or wrap in waxed paper, then serve.

Chicago Deep-dish Pizza

Every year I take a trip to Chicago for the big St. Patrick's Day parade and my trip is never complete until I indulge in a traditional Chicago-style pizza. Unfortunately, I could only enjoy it once a year. So you know how I took care of that? I made my own version, how else?!

6 TO 8 SLICES

1 pound hot Italian sausage,
  casings removed
  (see Helpful Hints)
1 medium green bell pepper,
  cut into ¼-inch strips
1 small onion, chopped
1 pound store-bought pizza
  dough
¾ cup pizza or spaghetti sauce
1½ cups (6 ounces) shredded
  mozzarella cheese

HELPFUL HINTS

Not crazy about the hot stuff? Use a milder sausage for the same super Chicago taste.

Preheat the oven to 450°F. Coat a 12-inch deep-dish pizza pan with nonstick cooking spray. In a large skillet, cook the sausage, pepper, and onion over medium heat for 6 to 8 minutes, or until no pink remains in the sausage and the vegetables are tender, stirring constantly; drain and set aside. Using your fingertips or the heels of your hands, spread the dough so that it covers the bottom of the pan and comes three quarters of the way up the sides. Spread the spaghetti sauce over the dough; top with the sausage mixture, then the cheese. Bake for 20 to 25 minutes, or until the crust is crisp and brown. Cut and serve.

BEEF

King-Cut Prime Rib

Who says we need to go to a restaurant when we feel like having a nice juicy prime rib? We don't! Did you know that it's one of the easiest dishes to make? Sure, 'cause the oven does all the work and all we do is simply carve and enjoy.

---

6 TO 8 SERVINGS

One 4- to 4½-pound boneless
   beef rib eye roast
1 teaspoon butter, melted
½ teaspoon garlic powder
½ teaspoon onion powder
2 teaspoons salt
2 teaspoons black pepper
½ cup mayonnaise
⅓ cup prepared white
   horseradish, drained
1 teaspoon lemon juice
¼ teaspoon white pepper

TIPS FROM THE PROS

Prime rib is often roasted on a bed of vegetables, allowing air to circulate around the beef as it cooks and extract the maximum flavor from the veggies. If you make it this way, be sure to discard the vegetables after cooking.

Preheat the oven to 350°F. Place the beef fat side up in a large roasting pan. In a small bowl, combine the melted butter, garlic powder, onion powder, salt, and black pepper; mix well and rub over the surface of the beef. Roast for 1½ to 1¾ hours, or until a meat thermometer inserted in the center reaches 140°F. for medium-rare, or until desired doneness beyond that. Meanwhile, in a small bowl, combine the remaining ingredients; mix well, cover, and chill for at least 30 minutes. Remove the prime rib to a cutting board and let stand for 15 to 20 minutes, then slice across the grain into thick slices and serve with the horseradish sauce.

Country-Fried Steak

True country-fried steak is made in a cast-iron skillet using cracklings or left-over pieces of fat. If that sounds a little messy to you, why not make this tasty but easier and neater version?

4 SERVINGS

4 beef cubed steaks (1¼ pounds total), pounded to a ¼-inch
   thickness
1¼ teaspoons salt, divided
¾ teaspoon black pepper
¾ cup buttermilk
¾ cup plus 3 tablespoons flour, divided
½ cup vegetable shortening
1½ cups milk

Season the cubed steaks with ¾ teaspoon salt and ½ teaspoon pepper; set aside. Place the buttermilk in a shallow dish. Place ¾ cup flour in another shallow dish. Dip the steaks in the buttermilk, then in the flour, coating completely. In a large skillet, heat the shortening over medium-high heat until hot but not smoking. Add 2 steaks and cook for 3 to 4 minutes per side, or until cooked through and the coating is golden. Drain on a paper towel–lined platter and cover to keep warm. Repeat with the remaining steaks. Add the remaining 3 tablespoons flour, ½ teaspoon salt, and ¼ teaspoon pepper to the skillet. Cook for 2 to 3 minutes, or until the flour is browned, stirring constantly. Add the milk and stir until the gravy thickens. Serve the steaks topped with the gravy.

Tangy Sauerbraten

Here's a simplified version of a traditional German favorite that you'll enjoy making and serving at home.

6 TO 8 SERVINGS

2 medium onions, thinly sliced
1 can (12 ounces) ginger ale
⅓ cup fresh lemon juice
¼ cup balsamic vinegar
2 tablespoons pickling spices
2 tablespoons sugar
2 garlic cloves, minced
½ teaspoon salt
¼ teaspoon black pepper
One 2- to 2½-pound boneless beef rump roast, cut across the
    grain into ¼-inch slices
1½ cups crushed gingersnap cookies
1 cup water

In a large resealable plastic storage bag, combine the onions, ginger ale, lemon juice, vinegar, pickling spices, sugar, garlic, salt, and pepper; mix well. Add the meat, seal, and marinate in the refrigerator for at least 4 hours or overnight, turning the bag over occasionally. Transfer the beef and marinade to a large deep skillet and bring to a boil over medium-high heat. Cover and cook for 20 to 30 minutes, until the meat is tender. Remove the beef from the skillet; set aside. Strain the liquid and return it to the skillet. Add the crushed gingersnaps and water; cook over medium-low heat until the gingersnaps dissolve and the sauce is thickened. Return the beef to the skillet and heat through. Serve immediately.

Diner Salisbury Steak

Ever go to a diner and have a dish with an ingredient that you just can't seem to identify? It might be a spice or an herb, but the flavor definitely stands out. In this dish, the horseradish is what adds the extra zing that makes it so special.

4 SERVINGS

1¼ to 1½ pounds ground beef
1 small onion, finely chopped
¼ cup seasoned bread crumbs
1 egg
2 tablespoons chopped fresh
   parsley
1 teaspoon prepared white
   horseradish, drained
1 teaspoon salt
¼ pound sliced fresh mushrooms
1 can (10½ ounces) mushroom gravy

TIPS FROM THE PROS

For a more traditional Salisbury steak, sprinkle a bit of crumbled cooked bacon over the meat during the last few minutes of cooking.

Coat a large skillet with nonstick cooking spray. In a medium bowl, combine all the ingredients except the mushrooms and gravy. Mix thoroughly and shape into 4 oval patties about ½ inch thick. Heat the skillet over medium heat; place the patties in the skillet and cook for 6 to 7 minutes per side, or until no pink remains. Remove to a platter and cover with aluminum foil to keep warm. Drain off all but 1 tablespoon of the liquid from the pan. Sauté the mushrooms over medium heat for 3 to 5 minutes, or until tender. Add the gravy and heat for 3 to 4 minutes, or until heated through. Return the Salisbury steaks to the skillet and cook until heated through. Serve the steaks topped with the mushroom gravy.

Old-fashioned Meat Loaf

Meat loaf has become so trendy that we find it on menus everywhere from diners to fancy restaurants. Each place prepares it a different way, but my favorite version is this one topped with a sweetened caramelized glaze of ketchup and brown sugar. Mmm, mmm!

6 TO 8 SERVINGS

2 pounds ground beef
1 onion, finely chopped
1 green bell pepper, finely chopped
1 egg
¾ cup Italian-flavored bread crumbs
1 cup ketchup, divided
½ teaspoon black pepper
1 tablespoon brown sugar

Preheat the oven to 350°F. Coat a 9" × 5" loaf pan with nonstick cooking spray. In a large bowl, combine the ground beef, onion, green pepper, egg, bread crumbs, ¾ cup ketchup, and the black pepper. Using your hands, mix the ground beef mixture well; place in the loaf pan. Bake for 1 hour. Brush with the remaining ¼ cup ketchup, sprinkle with the brown sugar, and bake for 15 to 20 minutes more, or until no pink remains. Drain, if necessary, then slice and serve.

Classic Filet Mignon

If you've ever seen filet mignon on a menu and had no idea what it was . . . you're not alone! It's simply a nice cut of steak with a fancy name. You'll love each tender and juicy bite so much that it'll become a favorite in your kitchen.

---

4 SERVINGS

---

4 filet mignon steaks (6 to 8
   ounces each), about 1¼
   inches thick
¼ teaspoon salt
¼ teaspoon black pepper
4 slices bacon

TIPS FROM THE PROS

Use thick-cut bacon to give this extra-rich flavor.

Preheat the broiler. Season the steaks with the salt and pepper. In a large skillet, lightly cook the bacon over medium-high heat until lightly browned, but not crisp. Wrap 1 slice of bacon around each steak and secure with a wooden toothpick. Place the steaks on a broiler pan or rimmed baking sheet and broil for 5 to 6 minutes per side for medium-rare, or until desired doneness beyond that. Remove the toothpicks and serve.

Dinosaur Ribs

There are two kinds of barbecue in this world: wet and saucy Southern style, and dry rub style, also known as Memphis style. These large, beefy, juicy ribs combine the best of both lip-smackin' worlds and are sure to satisfy a dinosaur of an appetite.

4 TO 6 SERVINGS

1 tablespoon ground cumin
1 tablespoon dried oregano
1 tablespoon dried thyme
1 tablespoon chili powder
1 tablespoon garlic powder
6 to 7 pounds beef back ribs,
   trimmed and cut into
   individual ribs
¼ cup barbecue sauce

TIPS FROM THE PROS

To minimize oven cleanup, make sure to use a roasting pan that's large enough that the ribs don't hang over its sides.

Preheat the oven to 375°F. In a small bowl, combine the cumin, oregano, thyme, chili powder, and garlic powder; mix well. Line a large roasting pan with aluminum foil, then place a roasting rack in the pan. Coat the rack with nonstick cooking spray. Rub the seasoning mixture evenly over the ribs; place the ribs on the roasting rack, over-lapping them if necessary. Roast uncovered for 1 hour. Brush the ribs with the barbecue sauce and roast, uncovered, for 25 to 30 minutes more, or until the ribs are tender and cooked through. Serve immediately.

Beef Wellington

At fancy restaurants, beef Wellington usually has a hefty price tag attached. Here's my version that's just as tasty but won't dent our wallets.

---

4 SERVINGS

¼ pound fresh mushrooms, finely chopped
1 garlic clove, minced
½ teaspoon dried thyme, divided
1 package (17¼ ounces) frozen puff pastry (2 sheets), thawed
4 filet mignon steaks (4 to 5 ounces each), about 1 inch thick
½ teaspoon salt
¼ teaspoon black pepper
1 jar (12 ounces) beef gravy
¼ cup dry red wine
⅛ teaspoon dried tarragon

Preheat the oven to 425°F. Coat a large rimmed baking sheet with nonstick cooking spray. In a medium nonstick skillet, cook the mushrooms, garlic, and ¼ teaspoon thyme over medium heat for 6 to 8 minutes, or until the mushrooms are tender. Remove from the heat; set aside. Unfold the puff pastry sheets and cut each crosswise in half. Spoon the mushroom mixture onto the centers of the 4 pieces of puff pastry. Season both sides of the steaks with the salt and pepper; place over the mushroom mixture. Bring the corners of the pastry up over the steaks; using your fingers, pinch the corners and edges together to seal completely. Place seam side down on the baking sheet and bake for 20 to 25 minutes, or until the pastry is puffed and golden and the meat is cooked to desired doneness. Meanwhile, in the same skillet, combine the remaining ingredients. Bring to a boil over medium-high heat, stirring frequently. Serve the wine sauce over the Wellingtons.

Grilled Flank Steak

Most of us think that we can only enjoy the taste of our favorite grilled specialties in the summer or when the weather is warm. Not anymore, thanks to the availability of grill pans and ridged skillets. We can savor tasty delights like flank steak all year round.

4 TO 6 SERVINGS

½ cup olive oil
3 tablespoons red wine vinegar
1 scallion, thinly sliced
2 garlic cloves, minced
½ teaspoon salt
1 teaspoon black pepper
One 1¾- to 2-pound beef
    flank steak, about 1 inch
    thick

TIPS FROM THE PROS

Top the steak with a fresh tomato salsa
or caramelized red onions.

In a large resealable plastic storage bag, combine all the ingredients except the steak; mix well. Score the steak on both sides by making shallow diagonal cuts 1½ inches apart. Place the steak in the storage bag, seal, and marinate in the refrigerator for at least 4 hours, or overnight, turning the bag over occasionally. Heat a large grill pan over high heat until hot. Remove the steak from the marinade and place in the pan; discard the marinade. Cook for 4 to 5 minutes per side for medium-rare, or until desired doneness beyond that. Thinly slice the steak across the grain and serve.

Beef Stroganoff

My version of this dish has a yummy sauce that's made in half the time of the traditional long-cooked sauce.

4 TO 6 SERVINGS

1 tablespoon butter
1½ pounds boneless beef top sirloin steak, well trimmed and
    thinly sliced across the grain
1 small onion, chopped
½ pound sliced fresh mushrooms
1 can (10¾ ounces)
    condensed cream of
    mushroom soup
1 cup dry white wine
¼ teaspoon salt
¼ teaspoon black pepper
1 pound medium egg noodles
1 cup sour cream
2 tablespoons chopped fresh
    parsley

TIPS FROM THE PROS

Restaurants have an easy trick for slicing the steak: they place it in the freezer for an hour or so first so it freezes slightly.

Melt the butter in a large skillet over medium-high heat. Add the steak and onion and cook for 5 to 7 minutes, until the steak is browned and the onion is tender, stirring occasionally. Add the mushrooms and cook for 3 minutes, until tender. Reduce the heat to medium-low and stir in the soup, wine, salt, and pepper; simmer for 25 minutes, or until the steak is tender. Meanwhile, cook the noodles according to the package directions. Drain, then cover to keep warm; set aside. Add the sour cream and parsley to the steak mixture and cook for 1 minute, until heated through; do not boil. Serve over the warm noodles.

Cafeteria-Style Chili

When I think of chili, words like basic *and* hearty *come to mind. That's right, chili's not fancy, it's just a simple yet filling dish that's easy to make and even easier to enjoy. Why not serve up a bowl today?*

5 TO 6 SERVINGS

1 pound lean ground beef
1 medium onion, chopped
2 cans (15 ounces each) pinto
    beans, undrained
1 can (28 ounces) diced
    tomatoes, undrained
1 can (15 ounces) tomato
    sauce
1 can (4 ounces) chopped
    green chilies, undrained
2 tablespoons chili powder
1 teaspoon ground cumin
½ teaspoon salt
½ teaspoon black pepper

TIPS FROM THE PROS

Add a little hot pepper sauce or ground red pepper for a spicier chili. Serve in bowls topped with all the classic chili fixin's, like shredded cheese, sour cream, chopped onion, and sliced jalapeño peppers.

In a soup pot, brown the ground beef and onion over medium-high heat for 5 to 7 minutes. Add the remaining ingredients, reduce the heat to medium-low, and cook for 1 hour, or until the chili is thickened, stirring occasionally.

New York Strip Steak with Mushrooms

Here's a restaurant-style sauce you can serve anytime because it goes together so simply.

2 SERVINGS

5 tablespoons butter, divided
1 tablespoon all-purpose flour
½ pound thick-sliced fresh
    mushrooms
½ cup sherry
⅛ teaspoon browning and
    seasoning sauce (optional)
½ teaspoon black pepper,
    divided
2 boneless beef loin strip steaks
    (about 12 ounces each)
½ teaspoon salt

HELPFUL HINTS

I love the flavor of grilled steak, and a grill pan is a good alternative for getting that same kind of flavor indoors all year round, but in warm weather, by all means use an outdoor grill.

In a large skillet, melt 4 tablespoons butter over medium heat. Add the flour and mix well. Add the mushrooms and sauté for 3 to 5 minutes, or until golden brown. Stir in the sherry, the browning sauce, if desired, and ¼ teaspoon black pepper. Reduce the heat to low and cook for 5 to 6 minutes, or until the sauce is thickened, stirring occasionally. Meanwhile, heat a grill pan over high heat. Rub both sides of the steaks with the remaining 1 tablespoon butter and sprinkle with the salt and the remaining ¼ teaspoon pepper. Place the steaks in the grill pan and cook for 4 to 5 minutes per side for medium-rare, or until desired doneness beyond that. Serve the steaks topped with the mushroom-sherry sauce.

Chicken Française

You're likely to find this dish on the menu in restaurants serving many different types of cuisines. And when you make it yourself, everyone is bound to tell you, "C'est si bon!!" "Ah é molto bene!!" or, my personal favorite, "OOH IT'S SO GOOD!!®"

6 SERVINGS

½ cup all-purpose flour
1 tablespoon chopped fresh parsley
½ teaspoon salt
3 eggs
4 tablespoons (½ stick) butter
6 boneless, skinless chicken breast halves
    (1½ to 2 pounds total), pounded to a
    ¼-inch thickness
⅔ cup dry vermouth or white wine
Juice of 2 lemons

In a shallow dish, combine the flour, parsley, and salt; mix well. In another shallow dish, beat the eggs. Melt 1 tablespoon butter in a large skillet over medium heat. Dip the chicken in the flour mixture, then in the eggs, coating completely. Sauté the chicken, in batches if necessary, for 2 to 3 minutes per side, or until golden, adding more butter as needed. Add any remaining butter, the vermouth, and lemon juice to the pan; mix well and return the cooked chicken to the skillet. Cook for 2 to 3 minutes, or until the sauce begins to thicken slightly. Serve the chicken with the sauce.

Chicken Cordon Bleu

You certainly don't need a diploma from the Cordon Bleu cooking school in France to make this melt-in-your-mouth chicken classic. All you need is about 45 minutes and a hungry gang.

4 SERVINGS

1 egg
½ cup Italian-flavored bread crumbs
4 boneless, skinless chicken breast halves
  (1 to 1¼ pounds total), pounded to a ¼-inch thickness
¼ teaspoon salt
⅛ teaspoon black pepper
4 square slices (4 ounces) Swiss cheese
4 slices (¼ pound) deli ham
Nonstick cooking spray

Preheat the oven to 350°F. Coat a 7" × 11" baking dish with nonstick cooking spray. In a shallow dish, beat the egg. Place the bread crumbs in another shallow dish. Season the chicken with the salt and pepper. Place 1 cheese slice and 1 ham slice on top of each chicken breast. Roll up and secure each breast with a toothpick; dip in the beaten egg then in the bread crumbs, coating completely. Place the rolled chicken in the baking dish, then coat it lightly with nonstick cooking spray. Bake for 30 to 35 minutes, or until no pink remains in the chicken and the coating is golden. Remove the toothpicks and serve.

Chicken Kiev

A member of my test kitchen staff who once worked in the kitchen of a fancy country club likes to share their kitchen secrets with me. Apparently, when they prepared chicken Kiev it took hours to complete all the steps involved. My version's much easier . . . and oh so tasty, too!

6 SERVINGS

1 tablespoon dried parsley
1 tablespoon dried chives
½ teaspoon garlic powder
6 boneless, skinless chicken breast halves (1½ to 2 pounds total), pounded to a ¼-inch thickness
½ teaspoon salt
½ teaspoon black pepper
3 tablespoons butter, cut into 6 equal slices
1 tablespoon seasoned bread crumbs
⅛ teaspoon paprika

Preheat the oven to 350°F. Coat a 6-cup muffin tin with nonstick cooking spray. In a small bowl, combine the parsley, chives, and garlic powder; set aside. Season both sides of each chicken breast with the salt and pepper, then sprinkle 1 teaspoon of the parsley mixture on one side of each breast. Place a slice of butter in the center of each piece of chicken and tightly roll up each breast, tucking in the sides as you roll. Place the rolls seam side down in the muffin tins and sprinkle with the bread crumbs and paprika. Bake for 25 to 30 minutes, or until no pink remains and the juices run clear. Serve immediately.

Honey Chicken

A viewer wrote in asking me how to make honey chicken. It seems she thought she could simply pour honey over chicken and bake it just like that. She was so disappointed when it didn't taste the way she expected! Well, there's more to this dish than just honey and chicken—but not too much. Take a look . . .

4 TO 6 SERVINGS

⅓ cup sesame seeds

1 cup all-purpose flour

1½ teaspoons baking powder

½ teaspoon salt

¾ cup water

Vegetable oil for frying

1½ pounds boneless, skinless chicken breasts, cut into 1-inch chunks

½ cup honey

2 garlic cloves, minced

⅛ teaspoon soy sauce

In a large deep skillet, toast the sesame seeds over medium-high heat until golden. Remove from the skillet and set aside. In a large bowl, combine the flour, baking powder, salt, and water; mix well. Heat ¼ inch oil in the large skillet over medium heat until hot but not smoking. Dip the chicken pieces in the batter, coating completely. Cook the chicken in batches for 2 to 3 minutes per side, or until golden. Drain on a paper towel–lined platter. Meanwhile, in a medium saucepan, warm the remaining ingredients (except the sesame seeds) over low heat for 4 to 6 minutes. In a large bowl, combine the chicken, honey sauce, and sesame seeds; toss until well mixed and serve immediately.

Chicken Fingers

Whenever my whole family goes out to eat, we can always count on a few of the grandchildren ordering chicken fingers. Another thing we can almost always count on? A few of us adults snitching a finger or two when the kids aren't looking!

4 TO 6 SERVINGS

½ cup milk

1 egg

1 cup all-purpose flour

1 tablespoon confectioners' sugar

1 tablespoon salt

½ teaspoon black pepper

2 pounds boneless, skinless chicken breasts, cut into 1-inch strips

1 cup vegetable oil

TIPS FROM THE PROS

The oil must be hot before you add the chicken, so test it by dropping a little of the flour mixture into it. If you hear it sizzle, it's hot enough to add the chicken. Restaurants often serve these with bowls of dipping sauces in flavors like barbecue and honey-mustard.

In a small bowl, combine the milk and egg; beat well. In a medium bowl, combine the flour, sugar, salt, and pepper; mix well. Dip the chicken in the egg mixture, then in the flour mixture, coating completely. Heat the oil in a large skillet over medium heat until hot but not smoking. Add the chicken in batches and cook for 4 to 5 minutes per side, or until no pink remains and the coating is golden. Remove to a paper towel–lined platter to drain. Serve immediately.

Oven-Roasted Chicken

Ever wished you could make moist and juicy restaurant-style roasted chicken? All you need are some spices and a can of ginger ale. Yup, the ginger ale keeps it tender and, because you cook the chicken on the soda can, it roasts evenly, just like it does when it's cooked on a fancy rotisserie.

3 TO 4 SERVINGS

1 tablespoon vegetable oil
1 teaspoon paprika
1 teaspoon onion powder
1 teaspoon garlic powder
¾ teaspoon salt
½ teaspoon black pepper
1 can (12 ounces) ginger ale
One 3- to 3½-pound chicken

Preheat the oven to 400°F. Line a roasting pan with aluminum foil. In a small bowl, combine the oil, paprika, onion powder, garlic powder, salt, and pepper; mix well. Open the can of ginger ale and place it on a flat roasting rack in the roasting pan. Rub the seasoning mixture over the chicken, coating completely. Place the chicken, cavity down, over the soda can. Carefully place it in the oven and roast for 60 to 70 minutes, or until the chicken is no longer pink and the juices run clear. Carefully remove the chicken from the can; carve and serve.

Chicken Cacciatore

The secret to this dish is simple—use lots of fresh veggies for extra-fresh taste.

4 TO 6 SERVINGS

⅓ cup olive oil
½ pound sliced fresh mushrooms
2 bell peppers (1 red and 1 green), thinly sliced
1 large onion, cut in half, then cut into ¼-inch slices
½ cup all-purpose flour
½ teaspoon salt
¼ teaspoon black pepper
One 3- to 3½-pound chicken, cut into 8 pieces
1 jar (26 ounces) spaghetti sauce
1 large tomato, chopped
¼ cup water
¼ cup white wine (optional)

TIPS FROM THE PROS

This is often served over a bed of egg noodles and sprinkled with grated Parmesan cheese.

Heat the oil in a soup pot over medium-high heat. Add the mushrooms, bell peppers, and onion and cook for 3 to 4 minutes, or until just tender. Using a slotted spoon, remove the vegetables to a medium bowl, leaving any remaining oil in the pot. Meanwhile, combine the flour, salt, and pepper in a shallow dish; dip the chicken into the flour mixture one piece at a time, coating completely. In the same pot, cook the chicken pieces for 6 to 8 minutes per side, or until browned. Return the vegetables to the pot and add the remaining ingredients; mix well. Reduce the heat to medium-low and cook for 30 to 40 minutes, or until the chicken is tender and no pink remains. Serve the chicken topped with the sauce and vegetables.

Extra-Crispy Fried Chicken

Many fast-food restaurants fry their chicken in pressure cookers—and you could do that with this recipe if you want to by simply following the instructions for your pressure cooker. But if you don't have a pressure cooker, you can do it this way—in a skillet. Either way, you'll surely be enjoying yummy fried chicken in no time!

3 TO 4 SERVINGS

½ cup milk
1 egg
One 3- to 3½-pound chicken,
   cut into 8 pieces
1 cup all-purpose flour
1 tablespoon salt
1 teaspoon black pepper
3 cups vegetable oil

TIPS FROM THE PROS

Many fast food restaurants add MSG to their fried chicken. Since many people are sensitive to MSG, my homemade version doesn't use it—and I think it's every bit as tasty, and fresher tasting.

In a large bowl, combine the milk and egg; beat well. Add the chicken, coating completely. In another large bowl, combine the flour, salt, and pepper; mix well. Remove the chicken from the milk mixture and place in the flour mixture, coating completely. Heat the oil in a large deep skillet over medium heat until hot but not smoking. Carefully place the chicken in the oil and cook, turning occasionally, for 20 to 22 minutes, or until the coating is brown and the chicken is no longer pink. Drain on a paper towel–lined platter. Serve immediately.

Blackened Chicken

New Orleans is known for festivals, fun, and, most of all . . . food! Étouffées, po'boys, and blackened fish and chicken are favorites of that region. Instead of traveling to the Big Easy, why not make this Bourbon Street specialty in your own kitchen?

6 SERVINGS

2 teaspoons paprika
1 teaspoon dried thyme
½ teaspoon sugar
½ teaspoon onion powder
½ teaspoon garlic powder
¼ teaspoon ground red pepper
½ teaspoon salt
½ teaspoon black pepper
6 boneless, skinless chicken breast halves (1½ to 2 pounds total), pounded to a ¼-inch thickness

HELPFUL HINTS

This seasoning blend can also be used with fish or beef to create other favorite blackened dishes.

In a small bowl, combine all the ingredients except the chicken; mix well. Sprinkle the chicken with the seasoning mixture until completely coated. Heat a large skillet (cast-iron works best) over high heat until hot. Carefully place the chicken in the skillet in batches if necessary, and cook for 3 to 4 minutes per side, or until the coating is blackened and the chicken is no longer pink. Serve immediately.

Chicken Fricassee

If you plan on serving this restaurant favorite, you'd also better be ready with lots of fluffy white rice and a hearty appetite.

4 TO 6 SERVINGS

2 tablespoons vegetable oil
One 3- to 3½-pound chicken, cut into 8 pieces
1 large onion, chopped
2 carrots, coarsely chopped
1 can (10¾ ounces) condensed cream of celery soup
½ cup milk
1 tablespoon fresh lemon juice
¼ teaspoon dried thyme
1 bay leaf
½ teaspoon salt
¼ teaspoon black pepper

Heat the oil in a large skillet over medium-high heat. Add the chicken and cook for 5 to 6 minutes until brown on all sides, turning occasionally. Remove the chicken to a platter; drain off the excess fat from the skillet. Add the onion and carrots to the skillet and sauté for 3 to 4 minutes, or until the onion is tender. Meanwhile, in a small bowl, combine the soup, milk, lemon juice, thyme, bay leaf, salt, and pepper; mix well. Return the chicken to the skillet, then pour the soup mixture over the top. Reduce the heat to low, cover, and simmer for 45 to 50 minutes, or until the chicken is no longer pink and the juices run clear. **Remove and discard the bay leaf before serving.**

Sizzling Chicken Fajitas

When I go to a Mexican restaurant, I love to order fajitas. But there's often a problem with that: There's not enough room on the table for all that food! There's a dish for the meat and veggies, a container for the tortillas, and, of course, the salsa, guacamole, and other toppings. When we make fajitas at home, it's a lot easier to spread out and really enjoy them.

6 FAJITAS

3 tablespoons vegetable oil, divided
2 large onions, each cut into 8 wedges
2 large bell peppers (1 red and 1 green),
    cut into ½-inch strips
1 pound boneless, skinless
    chicken breasts, cut into
    ¼-inch strips
1 teaspoon garlic powder
½ teaspoon salt
½ teaspoon black pepper
Juice of 1 lime
Six 8-inch flour tortillas

TIPS FROM THE PROS

Serve these with the traditional fajita fixin's of shredded lettuce and cheese, chopped tomatoes, salsa, sour cream, and guacamole.

Heat 2 tablespoons oil in a large skillet over medium-high heat. Add the onions and bell peppers and sauté for 10 to 12 minutes, or until the onions are lightly browned; remove to a bowl and set aside. Heat the remaining 1 tablespoon oil in the skillet and add the chicken, garlic powder, salt, and black pepper. Sauté for 5 to 6 minutes, or until the chicken is no longer pink. Return the vegetables to the skillet and cook for 3 to 5 minutes, stirring occasionally. Pour the lime juice over the chicken and vegetables; mix well. Divide the chicken mixture equally among the tortillas and serve.

Duck à l'Orange

The secret to perfectly cooked duck is to prick the skin all over with a fork before cooking. That way, the fat drains out and you're left with a juicy and flavorful main course like this one!

2 SERVINGS

One 3½- to 4-pound duck, cut
  in half (see Helpful Hints)
1 tablespoon plus 2 teaspoons
  salt, divided
1 teaspoon black pepper
1 jar (12 ounces) orange
  marmalade
1 can (11 ounces) mandarin
  oranges, drained
⅛ teaspoon ground red pepper

HELPFUL HINTS

If the duck is frozen when purchased, ask the butcher to cut it in half for you.

Preheat the oven to 450°F. Season the duck on both sides with 1 tablespoon salt and the pepper. Place on a rack in a roasting pan and prick the skin all over with a fork. Roast for 45 minutes. Meanwhile, in a medium bowl, combine the marmalade, the remaining 1 teaspoon salt, the mandarin oranges, and ground red pepper; mix well. Remove the duck from the oven and spread ½ cup of the marmalade mixture over it; reserve the remaining mixture. Reduce the oven temperature to 350°F. and bake for 25 to 30 minutes, or until the juices run clear or a meat thermometer inserted in the center reads 165°F. Serve the duck topped with the remaining sauce.

Seared Pork Tenderloin

If a restaurant menu includes pork tenderloin, don't pass it by. It's absolutely the best cut of pork. Why not try it yourself at home if you need convincing . . . ?

4 TO 6 SERVINGS

1 tablespoon vegetable oil
2 pork tenderloins (1½ to 2 pounds total)
½ teaspoon rubbed sage
½ teaspoon salt
¼ teaspoon black pepper
1 garlic clove, minced
⅓ cup water
1 tablespoon chopped fresh parsley

In a large skillet, heat the oil over high heat. Rub the tenderloins with the sage, salt, and pepper. Add to the skillet and brown on all sides. Add the garlic and water, then reduce the heat to medium-low, cover, and cook for 15 to 17 minutes, or until desired doneness. Sprinkle with the parsley, cut into thin slices, and serve with the pan drippings.

Sweet-and-Sour Pork

I found that if we coat our raw pork with cornstarch instead of flour, it makes for a crispier coating. That's just another one of those little tips that restaurant chefs don't usually share!

4 TO 6 SERVINGS

1 tablespoon vegetable oil
1 tablespoon cornstarch
½ teaspoon salt
¼ teaspoon ground red pepper
2 to 2½ pounds boneless pork
    sirloin, cut into bite-sized
    pieces
2 green bell peppers, cut into
    ½-inch strips
1 can (8 ounces) pineapple
    chunks, undrained
1 cup sweet-and-sour sauce

TIPS FROM THE PROS

This looks great topping a large plate piled high with steaming white rice and garnished with maraschino cherries.

Heat the oil in a large skillet over high heat. Meanwhile, in a medium bowl, combine the cornstarch, salt, and ground red pepper; mix well. Add the pork and toss to coat. Add the pork to the skillet and sauté for 10 to 12 minutes, or until golden brown and no pink remains. Add the bell peppers, pineapple chunks, and sweet-and sour sauce; cook for 5 to 7 minutes, or until the peppers are crisp-tender and the sauce is hot. Serve immediately.

Stuffed Pork Chops

How do the restaurants keep their stuffed pork chops so moist? The secret is to start with really moist stuffing and not to overcook the chops. Follow these tips, and I guarantee you'll enjoy moist stuffed chops every time.

4 SERVINGS

2 cups corn bread stuffing
1 large rib celery, finely
chopped
1 small onion, finely chopped
¼ cup (½ stick) butter,
melted
¼ cup water
2 tablespoons chopped fresh
parsley
½ teaspoon salt, divided
½ teaspoon black pepper, divided
4 pork loin chops (about 1½ pounds total), about 1 inch thick
Nonstick cooking spray

Coating the chops with nonstick cooking spray helps them get nice and golden.

Preheat the oven to 350°F. Coat a 9" × 13" baking dish with nonstick cooking spray. In a medium bowl, combine the stuffing, celery, onion, butter, water, parsley, ¼ teaspoon salt, and ¼ teaspoon pepper; mix well. Cut a deep pocket into the side of each pork chop. Season the chops with the remaining ¼ teaspoon each salt and pepper and stuff each one with an equal amount of the corn bread mixture. Place the chops in the baking dish and coat with the nonstick cooking spray. Bake for 50 to 60 minutes, or until golden and cooked through. Serve.

Barbecued Baby Back Ribs

The longer these ribs bathe in the savory barbecue sauce the better. So plan ahead to coat them with the barbecue sauce, wrap them in foil, and refrigerate for up to 24 hours. Then oven-roast them as directed. You know, roasting them wrapped in foil is what makes them so darned tender.

2 TO 4 SERVINGS

2 racks pork baby back ribs (about 4 pounds total)
1 cup barbecue sauce, divided

Preheat the oven to 375°F. Place each rack of ribs on a piece of aluminum foil large enough to wrap it completely. Brush the ribs with ½ cup of the barbecue sauce, covering them completely, then wrap tightly in the foil. Place on rimmed baking sheets and bake for 1 hour, or until fork-tender. Remove from the oven and preheat the broiler. Carefully unwrap the ribs and remove the foil. Return the ribs to the baking sheets; brush with the remaining ½ cup barbecue sauce, covering them completely. Broil for 5 minutes per side, or until the sauce begins to brown. Cut into individual ribs and serve.

Pork Egg Foo Yung

Don't let the name scare you! Egg foo yung is simply a cousin to an omelet, frittata, or crêpe. And this tasty pork version makes a super anytime change-of-pace main course.

3 TO 4 SERVINGS

8 eggs
1 can (4 ounces) mushroom stems and pieces, drained and
   coarsely chopped
½ pound fresh bean sprouts, coarsely chopped
¼ pound thick-sliced deli roast pork, coarsely chopped
3 scallions, thinly sliced
¼ teaspoon salt
¼ teaspoon black pepper
About 4 tablespoons peanut oil
1 can (10½ ounces) chicken gravy
2 teaspoons soy sauce
1 teaspoon ground ginger

In a large bowl, beat the eggs. Add the mushrooms, bean sprouts, pork, scallions, salt, and pepper; mix well and set aside. Heat 1 tablespoon oil in a large nonstick skillet over high heat. Spoon three ¼-cup measures of the egg mixture into the skillet to form pancakes and cook for about 1 minute per side, or until golden. Remove to a serving platter and cover to keep warm. Repeat until all the egg mixture has been cooked, adding more oil to the skillet as needed. Combine the gravy, soy sauce, and ginger in the skillet over medium heat; mix well for 1 minute, or until heated through. Serve the pancakes topped with the gravy.

Steaming Pork Fried Rice

The #1 rule at so many restaurants is "Thou Shall Not Waste." This should hold true in your kitchen as well, so here's a throw-together meal using left-over pork and rice. With leftovers like these, who needs to call for take-out?

4 TO 6 SERVINGS

4 tablespoons peanut oil, divided
2 eggs, lightly beaten
½ pound cooked boneless pork loin, cut into small pieces
   (about 1 cup)
4 cups cold cooked rice
6 scallions, thinly sliced
1 cup frozen peas, thawed
3 tablespoons soy sauce
½ teaspoon sugar
½ teaspoon salt

Heat 1 tablespoon oil in a large skillet over high heat. Add the eggs and stir to scramble for 1 to 2 minutes, or until fluffy; remove from the skillet and set aside. Add the remaining 3 tablespoons oil to the skillet and heat. Add the pork, rice, and scallions and sauté for 3 to 4 minutes, or until well coated with oil. Return the scrambled eggs to the skillet and add the remaining ingredients. Cook for 3 to 4 minutes, or until heated through. Serve immediately.

Ham Steak with Raisin Sauce

Go back a few years, and many a restaurant regularly served up thick-cut ham steaks smothered with a tangy raisin sauce. Today it's become more of a holiday favorite. Now that we know how the restaurants do it, we can turn any night of the week into an extra-special holiday.

4 TO 6 SERVINGS

Two 1-pound ham steaks
1 cup apple juice
¼ cup packed light brown sugar
1 tablespoon cornstarch
1 teaspoon dry mustard
½ cup raisins

Preheat the oven to 350°F. Coat a 9" × 13" baking dish with nonstick cooking spray. Place the ham steaks in the baking dish. In a small bowl, combine the remaining ingredients; mix well and pour over the ham steaks. Bake for 12 to 15 minutes per side, or until heated through and the sauce is thickened. Cut the ham into serving-sized portions and serve topped with the raisin sauce.

VEAL AND LAMB

Veal Marsala

Anyone who's walked into a commercial kitchen while the cooks were doing prep work has most likely heard lots of pounding. That's from the prep chefs tenderizing meat. And that's why restaurant veal cutlets are usually as tender as can be. Wanna know another good reason for all that pounding? The meat cooks faster, without shrinking!

4 TO 5 SERVINGS

¼ cup all-purpose flour
1 teaspoon salt
½ teaspoon black pepper
1 pound veal cutlets, pounded
    to a ¼-inch thickness
2 tablespoons olive oil
2 garlic cloves, minced
½ pound sliced fresh
    mushrooms (see Helpful
    Hints)
2 tablespoons butter
2 tablespoons chopped fresh parsley
1 cup sweet Marsala wine

HELPFUL HINTS
No fresh mushrooms? It's okay to use canned or even leave them out.

In a shallow dish, combine the flour, salt, and pepper; add the veal, turning to coat completely. Heat the oil in a large skillet over medium-high heat. Sauté the garlic and the veal for 2 to 3 minutes per side, until the veal is browned. Remove the veal to a platter; set aside. Add the mushrooms, butter, and parsley to the skillet and cook until the mushrooms are tender, stirring occasionally. Stir in the wine, then return the veal to the skillet and cook for 3 to 5 minutes, until the sauce is thickened and the veal is heated through. Serve immediately.

Osso Buco

You should expect to pay top dollar if you order this classic dish in a fancy restaurant. So I bet once you see how inexpensive it is to make at home, you'll be serving this flavor-packed dish again and again.

---

4 S E R V I N G S

⅓ cup all-purpose flour
½ teaspoon salt
½ teaspoon black pepper
4 cross-cut veal shanks (about 2½ pounds total)
3 tablespoons vegetable oil
1 can (10½ ounces) condensed beef broth
1 cup dry white wine
4 carrots, chopped
1 tomato, chopped
1 onion, chopped
2 garlic cloves, minced
2 tablespoons chopped fresh parsley
1 teaspoon grated lemon peel
2 tablespoons cornstarch
2 tablespoons water

In a shallow dish, combine the flour, salt, and pepper. Add the veal and coat completely. Heat the oil in a soup pot over medium-high heat. Add the veal and cook for 4 to 5 minutes per side, until browned. Add the broth, wine, carrots, tomato, onion, garlic, parsley, and lemon peel; bring to a boil. Reduce the heat to low, cover, and simmer for 1½ to 2 hours, until the veal is fork-tender, stirring occasionally. In a small bowl, combine the cornstarch and water; stir into the veal mixture until the sauce is thickened. Serve the veal topped with the sauce.

Special Veal Parmigiana

Some people insist on frying in vegetable oil, while others prefer butter. How about compromising and using both as in this recipe? You'll notice the difference when you cook it and when you taste it!

4 TO 5 SERVINGS

2 eggs
½ teaspoon salt
¼ teaspoon black pepper
1½ cups Italian-flavored bread crumbs
1 pound veal cutlets, pounded to a ¼-inch thickness
About ½ cup (1 stick) butter, divided
About ¼ cup vegetable oil
1½ cups spaghetti sauce, warmed
2 cups (8 ounces) shredded mozzarella cheese

TIPS FROM THE PROS

To make chicken Parmigiana, substitute boneless, skinless chicken cutlets for the veal.

Preheat the oven to 400°F. Coat a rimmed baking sheet with nonstick cooking spray. In a shallow dish, beat together the eggs, salt, and pepper. Place the bread crumbs in another shallow dish. Dip each veal cutlet in the egg mixture, then in the bread crumbs, coating completely; set aside. Melt 2 tablespoons butter with 2 tablespoons oil in a large skillet over medium heat. Add the veal in batches and cook for 1 to 2 minutes per side, or until golden, adding more butter and oil as needed. Drain on paper towels, then place on the coated baking sheet in a single layer. Spread the spaghetti sauce evenly over the veal, then sprinkle with the cheese. Bake for 3 to 4 minutes, or until heated through and the cheese is melted.

Veal Oscar

There have been lots of version of "Oscars," but the tried-and-true trophy winner is a veal medallion topped with chunks of crabmeat and a few asparagus spears, then smothered in a hard-to-make hollandaise sauce. Allow me to present this easy version that's sure to win you the dinner trophy!

6 SERVINGS

½ cup all-purpose flour
½ teaspoon salt
¼ teaspoon black pepper
6 veal cutlets (about 1 pound total), lightly pounded
About 2 tablespoons butter
1 package (10 ounces) frozen asparagus spears, thawed and
  drained
1 can (6½ ounces) lump crabmeat, drained and flaked
½ cup sour cream
½ cup mayonnaise
1 tablespoon yellow mustard
2 teaspoons fresh lemon juice

Preheat the oven to 450°F. In a shallow dish, combine the flour, salt, and pepper; mix well. Add the veal, turning to coat completely. Melt 1 tablespoon butter in a large skillet over medium heat. Add the veal in batches and sauté for 1 to 2 minutes, or until lightly golden, turning once and adding more butter as needed. Place the veal in a single layer in a 9" × 13" baking pan. Top each cutlet with an equal amount of asparagus and then crabmeat. In a small bowl, combine the remaining ingredients; mix well and spoon evenly over the crabmeat. Bake for 8 to 10 minutes, or until the sauce is bubbly and light golden. Serve immediately.

Peppery Veal Chops

One of the easiest ways to season meat is with a blend of seasonings called a rub. It forms a flavorful crust around the meat that's very "in" these days.

4 SERVINGS

2 teaspoons dry mustard

2 teaspoons garlic powder

1 teaspoon crushed red pepper

1 teaspoon salt

2 teaspoons cracked black
peppercorns or coarse-
ground black pepper

3 tablespoons vegetable oil

4 veal loin chops (about 2
pounds total)

Cook this in a heavy aluminum or cast-iron skillet to really sear the outside and seal in the juices.

In a small bowl, combine all the ingredients except the chops; mix well. Evenly rub the seasoning mixture over the chops. Heat a large dry skillet over medium heat. Add the veal chops and cook for 6 to 8 minutes per side, until browned, or until desired doneness. Serve.

Slow-Roasted Leg of Lamb

The trick to making a tender roast leg of lamb is to slow-roast it, then carve it across the grain. Yes, it's really that simple!

8 TO 10 SERVINGS

5 tablespoons butter, softened, divided
1 teaspoon garlic powder
1 teaspoon onion powder
½ teaspoon paprika
½ teaspoon dried thyme
1 teaspoon salt
¾ teaspoon black pepper, divided
One 6-pound boneless leg of lamb, tied
½ pound sliced fresh mushrooms
1 can (10½ ounces) mushroom gravy
½ cup milk
1 teaspoon cornstarch

Preheat the oven to 350°F. In a small bowl, combine 3 tablespoons butter, the garlic powder, onion powder, paprika, thyme, salt, and ½ teaspoon pepper. Evenly coat the lamb with the mixture then place it on a wire rack in a roasting pan. Roast for 2½ to 3 hours, until desired doneness. Remove to a serving platter; pour off the grease from the pan, reserving some of the drippings. Place the pan on the stovetop over high heat. Add the mushrooms and remaining 2 tablespoons butter; sauté the mushrooms for 3 to 4 minutes, until golden. Add the mushroom gravy, milk, cornstarch, and remaining ¼ teaspoon pepper; heat for 2 to 3 minutes, until hot and just thickened. Slice the lamb and serve topped with gravy.

Minty Lamb Chops

Most people simply roast or grill their meat with little or no seasoning and then wonder why it tastes so bland. The trick is to season the meat before roasting to bring out its natural flavor. That way, each and every bite is bursting with flavor.

4 SERVINGS

1 teaspoon garlic powder
1 teaspoon ground sage
1 teaspoon salt
½ teaspoon black pepper
2 pounds lamb loin chops
¼ cup mint jelly, melted

TIPS FROM THE PROS

Garnishing these with sprigs of fresh mint adds just the right finishing touch.

Preheat the oven to 400°F. Coat a rimmed baking sheet with nonstick cooking spray. In a small bowl, combine the garlic powder, sage, salt, and pepper; mix well, and season the lamb chops on both sides. Place on the baking sheet and bake for 20 to 25 minutes, to medium doneness, or until desired doneness beyond that. Top with the melted jelly and serve.

Lamb Kebabs

Some people might think that all skewers are created equal. Not true! You'll know after using the metal ones that are oval or flat, rather than round. Those don't let your meat slip off or twist around when you're cooking it on the grill or roasting it in the oven.

6 SERVINGS

Six 12-inch skewers
½ cup grated Parmesan cheese
2 garlic cloves, minced
1 teaspoon sugar
½ teaspoon ground cumin
½ teaspoon salt
½ teaspoon black pepper
3 pounds boneless leg of lamb,
    cut into twenty-four
    1½-inch chunks

TIPS FROM THE PROS

You can make this a true Middle Eastern delight by serving the kebabs over a bed of rice pilaf.

Preheat the broiler. If using wooden skewers, soak them in water for 15 minutes. In a large bowl, combine the cheese, garlic, sugar, cumin, salt, and pepper; mix well. Add the lamb chunks and toss to coat completely. Thread 4 lamb chunks onto each skewer, leaving space between the pieces. Place the skewers on a broiler pan or rimmed baking sheet and broil for 4 to 6 minutes per side, or until desired doneness. Serve immediately.

Simmering Curried Lamb

Authentic Indian restaurants don't use canned curry powder. Instead, they grind their own spice blends. Re-creating these true flavors is sure to take more time than most of us have, so with a few shakes here and a few shakes there, you can still have Indian dishes that are rich-tasting and close to the real thing.

4 TO 6 SERVINGS

1 tablespoon butter
2 medium onions, chopped
3 garlic cloves, minced
2 tablespoons all-purpose flour
2 tablespoons curry powder
¼ teaspoon ground ginger
¼ teaspoon ground red pepper
1 teaspoon salt
2 pounds boneless leg of lamb, cut into 1-inch chunks
1 can (15 ounces) coconut milk
1 package (9 ounces) frozen cut green beans, thawed

TIPS FROM THE PROS

This becomes a complete meal (a more attractive one, too!) served over a bed of rice and topped with cashew halves.

Melt the butter in a soup pot over medium heat. Add the onions and garlic and sauté for 3 to 4 minutes, or until tender, stirring occasionally. Meanwhile, in a large bowl, combine the flour, curry powder, ginger, ground red pepper, and salt; mix well. Add the lamb chunks and toss until well coated. Add the lamb to the soup pot and cook for 6 to 8 minutes, or until browned, stirring occasionally. Reduce the heat to medium-low; add the coconut milk and green beans and simmer for 10 to 15 minutes, or until the lamb is fork-tender. Serve immediately.

FISH AND SEAFOOD

Trout Amandine

Years ago, I tasted the most incredible trout with a sauce that was unbeliev-ably scrumptious. When I asked the chef what made the sauce so savory, he told me that he started it with fresh butter and browned the almonds in it to bring out more of their nutty flavor. Why not try it and see for yourself!

4 TO 6 SERVINGS

2 pounds trout fillets
¼ teaspoon salt
½ teaspoon black pepper
3 tablespoons butter
⅓ cup sliced almonds

Preheat the broiler. Coat a broiler pan or rimmed baking sheet with nonstick cooking spray. Season the fish fillets with the salt and pepper and place on the pan or baking sheet. Broil for 5 to 6 minutes, or until the fish flakes easily with a fork. Meanwhile, melt the butter in a medium skillet over medium-low heat. Add the almonds and cook for 2 to 3 minutes, or until golden. Top the broiled trout fillets with the almond butter and serve.

Light-as-Can-Be Fish Fry

There is a big difference between a good fish fry and a greasy fried fish. The first step is to make a good batter; then, it's even more important to fry the fish in high-quality peanut oil. Now that you know the trade secrets, follow these steps for a fantastic fish fry every time.

4 TO 6 SERVINGS

1½ cups all-purpose flour
1½ teaspoons baking powder
2 teaspoons sugar
2½ teaspoons salt
1 cup water
1 egg
Peanut oil for frying
2½ pounds cod fillets, cut into
    individual portions

TIPS FROM THE PROS

To complete the true fish fry experience, serve it on platters along with French fries and coleslaw. The secret to making restaurant-crisp French fries? Deep-fry raw potato strips in hot oil for 1 minute, then remove to a paper towel–lined plate until cool. Place the fries back in the hot oil and fry for 5 minutes, until golden and cooked through.

In a large bowl, combine the flour, baking powder, sugar, salt, water, and egg; mix well. Heat 1 inch of oil in a large deep skillet over medium heat until hot but not smoking. Dip the cod fillets into the batter, coating completely, then fry in the oil for 4 to 5 minutes per side, or until the coating is golden and the fish flakes easily with a fork. Drain on a paper towel–lined platter. Serve immediately.

Golden-Topped Salmon

The mayonnaise in this recipe makes such a super coating for the salmon that when you broil it, the fish looks like it magically puffs up! Voilà, it's a hit!

4 SERVINGS

⅓ cup mayonnaise
1 tablespoon fresh lemon juice
1 garlic clove, minced
1 teaspoon dried dillweed
¼ teaspoon salt
¼ teaspoon black pepper
4 salmon steaks (6 to 8 ounces each)

Preheat the broiler. Coat a broiler pan or rimmed baking sheet with nonstick cooking spray. In a small bowl, combine all the ingredients except the salmon; mix well. Spread the mixture evenly over the top of the salmon steaks. Place on the pan or baking sheet and broil for 12 to 15 minutes, or until the fish flakes easily with a fork. Serve immediately.

Crab-Stuffed Flounder

What makes one crab-stuffed flounder better than the next? From what I've learned, the crabmeat needs to be flaked well for the stuffing, and it should be mixed with mayonnaise for a moistness that'll set it apart from the rest.

6 SERVINGS

2 cans (6 ounces each) lump crabmeat, drained and flaked
1 cup Italian-flavored bread crumbs
1 rib celery, finely chopped
2 eggs
2 tablespoons mayonnaise
4 tablespoons (½ stick) butter, melted, divided
½ teaspoon Worcestershire sauce
¾ teaspoon black pepper, divided
6 flounder fillets (about 2 pounds total)
¼ teaspoon paprika

Preheat the oven to 350°F. Coat a 9" × 13" baking dish with nonstick cooking spray. In a medium bowl, combine the crabmeat, bread crumbs, celery, eggs, mayonnaise, 2 tablespoons melted butter, the Worcestershire sauce, and ¼ teaspoon pepper; mix well. Place the flounder fillets on a work surface and season with the remaining ½ teaspoon pepper. Spread the crabmeat stuffing equally down the center of each flounder fillet, roll up, and place seam side down in the baking dish. Brush with the remaining 2 tablespoons melted butter and sprinkle with the paprika. Bake for 25 to 30 minutes, or until the fish flakes easily with a fork. Serve immediately.

Catfish Fingers

Southern-style fried catfish has a particular taste that's often hard to imitate, but after lots of tries, I cracked the code. Combining eggs and sour cream as the base makes the cornmeal stick better and gives each finger a little extra flavor.

4 TO 6 SERVINGS

2 eggs
¼ cup sour cream
1½ teaspoons ground red pepper, divided
1½ teaspoons dried parsley, divided
1 teaspoon salt, divided
2 cups self-rising cornmeal
1½ cups vegetable oil
2 pounds catfish fillets, cut into 1-inch strips

In a shallow dish, whisk together the eggs, sour cream, ½ teaspoon ground red pepper, ½ teaspoon parsley, and ¼ teaspoon salt, blending well. In another shallow dish, combine the cornmeal and the remaining 1 teaspoon ground red pepper, 1 teaspoon parsley, and ¾ teaspoon salt; mix well. Heat the oil in a large skillet over medium-high heat until hot but not smoking. Meanwhile, dip the catfish fingers in the egg mixture, then in the cornmeal mixture, coating completely. Cook the catfish fingers in batches for 2 to 3 minutes per side, or until the coating is golden and the fish flakes easily with a fork. Drain on a paper towel–lined platter. Serve immediately.

Lobster Thermidor

4 SERVINGS

When you're looking for a really special dinner, this is the one. And there are no reservations required!

Four 6-ounce lobster tails, thawed if frozen
½ cup (1 stick) butter, divided
⅓ cup all-purpose flour
1 can (14½ ounces) ready-to-use chicken broth
⅔ cup heavy cream
½ teaspoon paprika
½ teaspoon black pepper
2 tablespoons sherry
½ cup plain bread crumbs

Using a knife or kitchen shears, carefully cut away and remove the underside of the lobster tail shells; remove the meat, reserving the remaining shells. Cut the lobster meat into 1-inch chunks. Melt ¼ cup butter in a large skillet over medium heat. Stir in the flour until well combined. Add the lobster meat, chicken broth, heavy cream, paprika, and pepper and cook for 5 to 6 minutes, or until the sauce thickens and the lobster turns opaque. Remove from the heat and stir in the sherry. Preheat the broiler. Place the empty lobster shells on a rimmed broiler pan or baking sheet and fill with the lobster mixture. In a small bowl, soften the remaining ¼ cup butter and mix with the bread crumbs. Sprinkle the bread crumb mixture over the lobster mixture and broil for 2 to 3 minutes, or until golden. Serve immediately.

Crispy Coconut Shrimp

Coconut shrimp is very popular at restaurants all along the East Coast. And why not? It's the perfect combination of sweet and savory sensations.

3 TO 4 SERVINGS

½ cup all-purpose flour
1 tablespoon sugar
1 teaspoon ground red pepper
½ teaspoon salt
2 eggs
2 tablespoons water
2½ cups sweetened flaked coconut
1 pound large shrimp, peeled, with tails left on, and deveined
2 cups vegetable oil

In a shallow dish, combine the flour, sugar, ground red pepper, and salt; mix well. In a medium bowl, beat together the eggs and water. Place the coconut in another shallow dish. Coat the shrimp with the flour mixture, then dip in the egg mixture. Roll in the coconut, pressing it firmly onto both sides of the shrimp to coat completely. Heat the oil in a large saucepan over medium heat. Cook the shrimp in batches for 1 minute per side, or until golden and cooked through. Drain on a paper towel–lined platter. Serve immediately.

Seafood Skewers

By mixing butter, lemon juice, and seasonings with bread crumbs, we get a rich topping for this dish that's sure to have your gang sending their compliments straight to the chef . . . you!

4 SERVINGS

Eight 12-inch wooden skewers
1¼ pounds jumbo shrimp, peeled, with tails left on, and deveined (see Tips from the Pros)
1¼ pounds sea scallops
½ cup (1 stick) butter, melted
2 tablespoons fresh lemon juice
¼ cup Italian-flavored bread crumbs
8 garlic cloves, minced
½ teaspoon paprika
¼ teaspoon salt

TIPS FROM THE PROS

Jumbo or colossal shrimp should be used here. Shrimp are classified according to the number there are in a pound. There are 12 to 15 jumbo shrimp to a pound and 16 to 20 colossal shrimp to a pound.

Soak the wooden skewers in water for 20 minutes. Preheat the broiler. Alternately thread the shrimp and scallops onto each skewer and place on a broiler pan or rimmed baking sheet. In a small bowl, combine the remaining ingredients; mix well. Spread half of the crumb mixture evenly on the top side of the shrimp and scallops; broil for 3 minutes. Turn the skewers and spread the remaining crumb mixture over the top. Broil for 3 minutes, or until the shrimp are pink and the scallops are no longer translucent. Serve immediately.

Shrimp Scampi Linguine

Did you know that most seafood restaurants give their seafood a squeeze of fresh lemon right before tossing with pasta? In fact, they use fresh lemon in so many of their recipes, and you can, too. Just remember—with lemon, a little goes a long way.

4 TO 6 SERVINGS

1 pound linguine
½ cup (1 stick) butter
1 tablespoon olive oil
1 pound medium shrimp, peeled, with tails left on, and deveined
12 garlic cloves, minced
1 teaspoon salt
½ teaspoon black pepper
½ cup dry white wine
2 tablespoons chopped fresh parsley
Juice of 1 lemon, optional

Cook the linguine according to the package directions; drain and keep warm in a serving bowl. Meanwhile, in a large skillet, melt the butter with the oil over medium-high heat. Add the shrimp and garlic, and season with salt and pepper; sauté for 2 to 3 minutes, until the shrimp are pink. Reduce the heat to low and add the wine, parsley, and lemon juice, if desired; simmer for 1 to 2 minutes. Add to the linguine, toss, and serve.

Broiled Seafood Platter

Many times we'll be in the mood for seafood but we just won't be able to decide exactly what we want. I guess that's why combination platters are so popular at seafood restaurants. If you make this platter the next time your gang is indecisive, you'd better be ready to reel in the compliments.

4 TO 6 SERVINGS

¼ cup (½ stick) butter, melted
3 garlic cloves, minced
Juice of ½ lemon
¼ teaspoon paprika
½ teaspoon salt
¼ teaspoon black pepper
2 pounds cod fillets
1¼ pounds large shrimp, peeled, with tails left on, and deveined
1 pound sea scallops

Preheat the broiler. In a medium bowl, combine the butter, garlic, lemon juice, paprika, salt, and pepper; mix well. Place the cod fillets on a broiler pan or rimmed baking sheet and brush with some of the butter mixture. Broil for 5 minutes. Add the shrimp and scallops to the broiler pan, brush with the remaining butter mixture, and broil for 8 to 10 minutes, or until the shrimp are pink, the scallops are no longer translucent, and the fish flakes easily with a fork. Divide equally among dinner plates and serve.

Golden Crab Cakes

You can make these large enough for a main course or bite-sized for a pre-dinner snack. But there's one thing to keep in mind: If you want them to be restaurant-special, be sure to use fresh (soft) bread crumbs.

8 ENTRÉE-SIZED PATTIES OR
16 APPETIZER-SIZED PATTIES

½ cup plain fresh (soft) bread crumbs (see Tips from the Pros)
½ cup mayonnaise
1 egg
2 tablespoons fresh lemon juice
1 tablespoon Worcestershire sauce
1 teaspoon Dijon-style mustard
2 scallions, thinly sliced
1 tablespoon chopped fresh parsley
1 teaspoon Old Bay Seasoning or other seafood seasoning
2 cans (6½ ounces each) lump crabmeat, drained
2 tablespoons butter

TIPS FROM THE PROS

To make fresh soft bread crumbs, toss a few slices of day-old bread into a food processor and process until finely crumbled.

In a medium bowl, combine all the ingredients except the crabmeat and butter; mix well. Fold in the crabmeat, being careful not to break up the crabmeat chunks. Form into 8 equal-sized patties if serving as a main course or 16 patties if serving as an hors d'oeuvre. Melt the butter in a large skillet over medium heat. Add the patties and sauté for 3 to 4 minutes per side, or until browned. Serve immediately.

Mussels Pomodoro

You can't get more Italian than mussels, tomatoes, and spaghetti. This dish is an Italian classic, bursting with rich, traditional flavors.

---

4 TO 6 SERVINGS

---

1 pound spaghetti
2 pounds mussels, cleaned (see
   Tips from the Pros)
1 can (14½ ounces) stewed
   tomatoes
¼ cup dry white wine
2 garlic cloves, minced
½ teaspoon dried oregano
1 teaspoon salt
¼ teaspoon black pepper

TIPS FROM THE PROS

If you buy mussels that aren't cleaned and ready for cooking, here's what to do: Wash them under cold running water and scrub away any grit or barnacles with a stiff food scrub brush. Remove the black "beard" from each mussel by cutting or pulling it off.

Cook the spaghetti according to the package directions; drain. Meanwhile, in a soup pot, combine the remaining ingredients over high heat; bring to a boil. Reduce the heat to low, cover, and cook for 2 to 3 minutes, or until the mussels open. **Discard any unopened mussels.** Serve the spaghetti in bowls topped with the mussels pomodoro.

Flash-Fried Oysters

Raw oysters on the half-shell are really popular, but these days, to play it safe, I prefer to eat my oysters cooked, and flash-frying them really highlights their flavor. I also recommend adding a dollop of spicy cocktail sauce and a squeeze of lemon juice to each one just before popping it into your mouth. Mmm, mmm!

3 TO 4 SERVINGS

2 eggs
1 tablespoon water
1 teaspoon salt
¼ teaspoon black pepper
1½ cups all-purpose flour
1 teaspoon ground red pepper
¾ cup vegetable oil
Two ½-pint containers (8 ounces each) shucked fresh oysters, rinsed and drained

In a shallow dish, combine the egg, water, salt, and pepper; beat well. In another shallow dish, combine the flour and ground red pepper; mix well. Heat the oil in a large skillet over medium-high heat. Dip the oysters in the egg mixture, then in the flour mixture, coating completely. Add to the skillet in batches and cook for 1 to 2 minutes per side, or until golden. Drain on a paper towel–lined platter. Serve immediately.

RESTAURANT PASTA FAVORITES

Penne Primavera

Pasta primavera became one of the most popular items on the menu at New York City's Le Cirque restaurant in the late '70s. Despite its fancy name, it's really a simple dish—just pasta and vegetables in a light sauce. Yes, it's simple, but so good!

6 TO 8 SERVINGS

1 pound penne pasta
¼ cup olive oil
2 yellow squash, cut into ½-inch chunks
1 large zucchini, cut into ½-inch chunks
1 red bell pepper, cut into ½-inch chunks
1 small onion, chopped
3 garlic cloves, minced
4 plum tomatoes, sliced
½ pound sliced fresh mushrooms
1 can (10½ ounces) condensed chicken broth
½ teaspoon salt
1 teaspoon black pepper
½ cup grated Parmesan cheese

In a soup pot, cook the pasta according to the package directions; drain in a colander and set aside. In the same pot, heat the oil over high heat. Add the yellow squash, zucchini, bell pepper, onion, and garlic and sauté for 8 minutes, until just tender. Add the tomatoes, mushrooms, chicken broth, salt, and black pepper and cook for 3 to 5 minutes, or until heated through. Return the pasta to the pot and cook until heated through, stirring frequently. Sprinkle with the cheese and serve.

Spaghetti with Red Clam Sauce

When cooking spaghetti or any other kind of pasta, be sure to cook it in a large pot of boiling salted water to keep it from becoming starchy-tasting. And be careful not to overcook your pasta. Boil it until it's al dente, which means it's still just a bit firm when you bite into it.

4 TO 6 SERVINGS

2 tablespoons olive oil
2 garlic cloves, minced
2 cans (10 ounces each) baby clams, undrained
1 jar (28 ounces) spaghetti sauce
2 tablespoons chopped fresh parsley
¼ teaspoon crushed red pepper
¼ teaspoon salt
⅛ teaspoon black pepper
1 pound spaghetti

Heat the oil in a medium saucepan over medium-high heat. Add the garlic and sauté for 1 to 2 minutes, or until golden. Add the remaining ingredients except the spaghetti; bring to a boil. Meanwhile, cook the spaghetti according to the package directions; drain. Serve the spaghetti topped with the clam sauce.

Capellini with White Clam Sauce

The secret to making clam sauce, whether it's red or white, is to use undrained cans of baby clams. The baby clams are easy to work with, and they give the sauce just the right fresh seafood taste. And since we eat with our eyes, you might want to garnish each plate with a few freshly steamed clams and lemon slices, just like the restaurants do.

4 TO 6 SERVINGS

2 tablespoons olive oil
2 garlic cloves, minced
2 cans (10 ounces each) baby clams, undrained
¼ cup dry white wine
2 teaspoons fresh lemon juice
¼ cup chopped fresh parsley
1 teaspoon salt
1 pound capellini (angel hair pasta)

Heat the oil in a medium saucepan over medium-low heat. Add the garlic and cook for 1 to 2 minutes, or until golden, stirring occasionally. Add the clams, wine, lemon juice, parsley, and salt and cook for 10 minutes, or until thoroughly heated. Meanwhile, cook the capellini according to the package directions; drain. Serve the capellini topped with the clam sauce.

Pesto Linguine

I used to wonder how restaurants kept their fresh pesto sauce so bright green, since, within a few hours of making mine, it would turn black. Then I found out that they squeeze some fresh lemon juice into the sauce to help it keep its bright color without really changing the taste.

4 TO 6 SERVINGS

2 cups lightly packed fresh
   basil leaves
1 cup olive oil
1 cup grated Parmesan cheese
2 garlic cloves
½ cup pine nuts or walnuts
½ teaspoon salt
1 tablespoon fresh lemon juice
1 pound linguine

TIPS FROM THE PROS

This is a dish that can't be beat when you serve it topped with freshly grated Parmesan cheese and a few toasted pine nuts.

In a blender or food processor, combine all the ingredients except the linguine; blend until smooth. Meanwhile, in a soup pot, cook the linguine according to the package directions; drain and return to the pot. Add the pesto sauce, toss until well combined, and serve.

Fettuccine alla Vodka

Since most of us don't get to Chicago's, Boston's, and New York's Italian sections as often as we'd like, I think I've managed to re-create that homemade flavor that's tops with almost any kind of pasta. So whip up some of your own sauce, dim the lights, open a bottle of wine, and enjoy!

4 TO 6 SERVINGS

1 tablespoon olive oil
3 garlic cloves, minced
¼ cup vodka
1 can (28 ounces) whole
   tomatoes, undrained,
   coarsely chopped
1 pound fettuccine
1 container (8 ounces)
   mascarpone cheese
   (see Helpful Hints)
2 tablespoons coarsely chopped fresh basil
1 teaspoon salt
1 teaspoon black pepper

HELPFUL HINTS

Mascarpone cheese is a soft, sweet Italian cheese similar in consistency to soft cream cheese. It is commonly used in dips and in sweet dishes like tiramisù (see page 170 for more info).

Heat the oil in a medium saucepan over medium heat. Add the garlic and sauté for 1 to 2 minutes, just until golden. Add the vodka and the tomatoes with their juice and bring to a boil. Reduce the heat to low and simmer for 15 minutes. Meanwhile, in a soup pot, cook the fettuccine according to the package directions. Drain, return the fettuccine to the pot, and cover to keep warm. Add the remaining ingredients to the tomato mixture and stir until thoroughly combined and the cheese is melted. Pour over the pasta and stir until combined, rewarming over low heat if necessary. Serve immediately.

Cold Sesame Noodles

You won't believe how much taste a bit of sesame oil gives this mouthwatering dish!

---

4 TO 6 SERVINGS

---

1 pound linguine or spaghetti
1 cup peanut butter
6 scallions, thinly sliced
2 tablespoons vegetable oil
2 tablespoons soy sauce
3 garlic cloves, minced
1½ teaspoons white vinegar
2 tablespoons sesame oil
¼ teaspoon ground red pepper

TIPS FROM THE PROS

Sure, you can serve this warm, but to bring out the sesame and peanut flavors, I suggest serving it cold, which is the traditional way. And to give it a restaurant-finished look, garnish with chopped peanuts and additional sliced scallions.

Cook the pasta according to the package directions; drain and set aside. In a large bowl, combine the remaining ingredients; mix well. Add the pasta and toss to coat evenly. Cover and chill for at least 1 hour before serving.

Eggplant Parmigiana

Okay, so there's no pasta in this recipe, but I've included it here because eggplant parmigiana isn't complete unless it's served alongside a big bowl of pasta with sauce.

6 TO 8 SERVINGS

4 eggs
½ teaspoon salt
¼ teaspoon black pepper
2 cups Italian-flavored bread crumbs
About ¾ cup olive oil
2 medium eggplant (about ¾ pound each), peeled and cut into
  ¼-inch slices
1 jar (28 ounces) spaghetti sauce
4 cups (16 ounces) shredded mozzarella cheese

Preheat the oven to 350°F. Coat a 9" × 13" baking dish with nonstick cooking spray. In a shallow dish, combine the eggs, salt, and pepper; beat well. Place the bread crumbs in another shallow dish. In a large skillet, heat 3 tablespoons oil over medium heat until hot but not smoking. Meanwhile, dip the eggplant slices in the egg mixture, then in the bread crumbs, coating completely. Place the coated eggplant slices in the skillet a few at a time and cook for 2 to 3 minutes per side, until golden, adding more oil as needed. Drain on paper towels. Spread 1 cup spaghetti sauce evenly over the bottom of the baking dish. Layer half of the cooked eggplant evenly over the sauce, overlapping as necessary. Cover the eggplant with half of the remaining spaghetti sauce and top with 2 cups cheese. Repeat the layers, then cover with aluminum foil and bake for 45 to 50 minutes, until hot and bubbly. Let sit for 10 minutes before serving.

Fettuccine Alfredo

This is absolutely an all-time favorite of mine. It's perfect for those times when you feel like having Italian food but want something other than a red sauce.

4 SERVINGS

12 ounces fettuccine
½ cup (1 stick) butter
2 cups (1 pint) heavy cream
½ teaspoon black pepper
1½ cups grated Parmesan
  cheese

TIPS FROM THE PROS

Many restaurants use this as the base for an even heartier dinner by topping each serving with a grilled chicken breast and some additional grated Parmesan cheese.

Cook the fettuccine according to the package directions; drain. Meanwhile, melt the butter in a large skillet over medium-low heat. Add the heavy cream and pepper; cook for 6 to 8 minutes, or until hot and well blended, stirring constantly. Stir in the cheese and cook for 6 to 7 minutes, or until the sauce is thickened. Pour the sauce over the fettuccine; toss and serve.

Stuffed Shells

How do restaurants manage to stuff their pasta shells so perfectly every time? The chefs use pastry bags—but you don't have to rush out and buy one. Nope! Just snip off a corner of a resealable plastic storage bag and use it the same way. It works just as well as the "professional" model!

6 TO 8 SERVINGS

12 ounces large pasta shells
1 container (32 ounces) ricotta cheese
3 cups (12 ounces) shredded mozzarella cheese, divided
½ cup plus 2 tablespoons grated Parmesan cheese, divided
2 eggs
1 tablespoon chopped fresh parsley
1 garlic clove, minced
1 teaspoon salt
½ teaspoon black pepper
1 jar (28 ounces) spaghetti sauce

Preheat the oven to 350°F. Coat a 9" × 13" baking dish with nonstick cooking spray. Cook the shells according to the package directions; drain. Meanwhile, in a large bowl, mix together the ricotta cheese, 2 cups mozzarella cheese, ½ cup Parmesan cheese, the eggs, parsley, garlic, salt, and pepper. Spread 1 cup spaghetti sauce evenly over the bottom of the baking dish. Fill each shell generously with the cheese mixture, about 1 tablespoon per shell, then place in the baking dish. Pour the remaining spaghetti sauce over the top. Sprinkle with the remaining 1 cup mozzarella and 2 tablespoons Parmesan cheese. Cover with aluminum foil and bake for 40 minutes. Remove the foil and bake for 8 to 10 minutes more, until the shells are heated through and the cheese is golden and bubbling. Let sit for 10 minutes before serving.

Worth-the-Wait Lasagna

When an oven-baked dish tastes this good, it's worth the wait!

6 TO 8 SERVINGS

12 lasagna noodles
1 pound bulk hot Italian sausage
4 cups (16 ounces) shredded mozzarella cheese, divided
1 container (15 ounces) ricotta cheese
⅓ cup grated Parmesan cheese
1 egg
½ teaspoon dried basil
½ teaspoon black pepper
2 jars (28 ounces each) spaghetti sauce

Preheat the oven to 375°F. Coat a 9" × 13" baking dish with nonstick cooking spray. Cook the noodles according to the package directions; drain. Meanwhile, in a large skillet, cook the sausage over medium-high heat until no pink remains, stirring to break up the meat as it cooks. Drain off the excess liquid and remove to a large bowl; let cool slightly. Add 3 cups mozzarella cheese, the ricotta and Parmesan cheeses, the egg, basil, and pepper; mix well. Spread 1 cup spaghetti sauce evenly over the bottom of the baking dish. Place 3 noodles over the sauce. Spread one third of the cheese mixture over the noodles. Pour 1 cup spaghetti sauce over the cheese mixture. Place 3 more noodles over the top and press down lightly. Repeat with 2 more layers of the cheese mixture, sauce, and noodles. Spoon the remaining sauce over the top and cover tightly with aluminum foil. Bake for 1 hour. Remove the foil and sprinkle the remaining 1 cup mozzarella cheese over the top; return to the oven for 5 minutes, or until the cheese is melted. Remove from the oven and allow to sit for 10 minutes before cutting and serving.

Rigatoni Bolognese

Marry *is a popular restaurant term that I like to use often myself. No, it doesn't involve rings or ceremonies. What it does involve is allowing adequate time for flavors to blend together . . . to end up with a taste that can't be beat.*

8 TO 10 SERVINGS

1 pound ground beef
1 green bell pepper, chopped
1 carrot, shredded
1 onion, chopped
1 garlic clove, minced
2 cans (15 ounces each) tomato sauce
1 beef bouillon cube
1 teaspoon sugar
1 teaspoon dried basil
1 teaspoon dried oregano
1½ pounds rigatoni pasta

In a soup pot, brown the beef over medium-high heat, stirring to break up the meat. Drain off the excess liquid and add the bell pepper, carrot, onion, and garlic. Cook for 4 to 5 minutes, or until the vegetables are tender, stirring occasionally. Add the remaining ingredients except the rigatoni, mix well, and bring to a boil. Reduce the heat to low, cover, and simmer for 20 minutes, allowing the flavors to marry, stirring occasionally. Meanwhile, cook the rigatoni according to the package directions; drain. Toss the rigatoni with the sauce and serve.

RESTAURANT
SIDE DISHES
FAVORITES

SIDE DISHES

Green Beans Amandine

Cooking fresh veggies in chicken broth is the easiest way to guarantee that they'll be packed with lots of juicy flavor. It's one of those little secrets restaurants don't rush to tell us, but that offer results we're sure to enjoy.

4 TO 6 SERVINGS

1 can (14½ ounces) ready-to-use chicken broth
1 pound fresh green beans, trimmed and cut into bite-sized
    pieces
¼ cup (½ stick) butter
½ cup sliced almonds
⅛ teaspoon black pepper

In a soup pot, bring the chicken broth to a boil over high heat. Add the green beans and return to a boil; cover and cook for 10 minutes, or until tender. Drain the green beans in a colander and set aside. Melt the butter in the soup pot; add the almonds and pepper and sauté over medium heat for 2 to 3 minutes, or until the almonds are golden. Add the green beans and toss to coat well; serve immediately.

Glazed Baby Carrots

Glazed baby carrots are a frequent tasty side dish at fancy hotel banquets. And now that you know how they make 'em, why not have a banquet at your house tonight?

4 TO 6 SERVINGS

2 tablespoons white vinegar
¼ teaspoon cornstarch
½ cup packed light brown sugar
2 tablespoons butter
2 cans (15 ounces each) whole baby carrots, drained

In a medium saucepan, combine the vinegar and cornstarch; mix until the cornstarch is dissolved. Add the brown sugar and butter and bring to a boil over medium heat, stirring until thickened. Add the carrots and cook for 3 to 5 minutes, or until heated through. Serve immediately.

Asparagus with Hollandaise Sauce

Of all the ways people make hollandaise sauce, this is not only the easiest but the most traditional. Even though hollandaise sounds like it must be difficult to make, it's really a simple restaurant-fancy sauce that you're gonna enjoy serving in your own dining room.

6 TO 8 SERVINGS

1 teaspoon salt
2 pounds fresh asparagus, trimmed
4 egg yolks
½ cup (1 stick) butter, melted
1 tablespoon fresh lemon juice
⅛ teaspoon black pepper

TIPS FROM THE PROS

To trim asparagus spears, simply snap off the cut (bottom) end of each with your hand at the point where it breaks naturally; that's where the tender part begins.

Fill a large skillet halfway with water; add the salt and bring to a boil over high heat. Add the asparagus and cook for 8 to 10 minutes, or until crisp-tender; drain. Meanwhile, in a small saucepan, beat the remaining ingredients until fluffy. Place over low heat and cook until thickened, stirring constantly. Serve the hollandaise sauce spooned over the asparagus.

Sweet Onion Tart

Here's a dish you're gonna rush to make when you really want to impress your gang.

---

6 TO 8 SERVINGS

One 9-inch frozen ready-to-bake pie shell, thawed
3 tablespoons butter
3 medium sweet onions, thinly sliced
2 eggs
1 cup sour cream
⅛ teaspoon dry mustard
½ teaspoon salt
⅛ teaspoon black pepper
⅛ teaspoon paprika

Preheat the oven to 350°F. Bake the pie shell for 8 to 10 minutes, or until light golden; set aside. Melt the butter in a medium skillet over high heat. Add the onions and sauté for 5 minutes. Reduce the heat to medium-low, cover, and sauté for 2 to 4 more minutes, or until tender. Place the sautéed onions in the pie shell. In a medium bowl, combine the eggs, sour cream, mustard, salt, and pepper; mix well and pour over the onions. Sprinkle the top with the paprika and bake for 40 to 45 minutes, or until the edges and crust are golden and a knife inserted in the center comes out clean. Cut into wedges and serve.

Spinach Soufflé

There's no need to tiptoe around the kitchen when this soufflé is in the oven. It's durable enough to stand up to the family, but fancy enough to serve to company.

4 TO 6 SERVINGS

1 cup (½ pint) heavy cream
3 eggs
2 packages (10 ounces each) frozen chopped spinach, thawed and squeezed dry
⅓ cup grated Parmesan cheese
2 tablespoons all-purpose flour
⅛ teaspoon ground nutmeg
⅛ teaspoon ground red pepper
½ teaspoon salt
¼ teaspoon black pepper

Preheat the oven to 350°F. Coat an 8-inch square baking dish with nonstick cooking spray. In a medium bowl, beat the heavy cream and eggs for 2 to 3 minutes, or until foamy. Add the remaining ingredients; mix well and pour into the baking dish. Bake for 30 to 35 minutes, or until a knife inserted in the center comes out clean. Cut into squares and serve.

Home-Style Black Beans

Authentic Cuban restaurants will spend more than a whole day preparing their black beans. They'll start by soaking dried beans overnight in a broth and the next day they'll add a variety of spices before simmering the beans for hours and hours. Instead of working that hard, try my quick shortcut version.

4 TO 6 SERVINGS

3 tablespoons olive oil
1 large green bell pepper,
   finely chopped
1 onion, chopped
6 garlic cloves, minced
2 cans (15 ounces each) black
   beans, undrained
1 cup water
2 tablespoons red wine vinegar
3 bay leaves

TIPS FROM THE PROS

These are traditionally served over white or yellow rice and topped with chopped onion.

Heat the oil in a medium saucepan over medium-high heat. Add the pepper and onion and sauté for 8 to 10 minutes, or until tender. Add the remaining ingredients and bring to a boil. Reduce the heat to medium and cook, uncovered, for 30 minutes. **Be sure to remove the bay leaves before serving**. Serve immediately.

Summer Veggies

Just as any leading actor needs a good supporting cast, an entrée needs tasty go-alongs to turn it into a complete meal. And here's one with the versatility to do the trick every time.

4 TO 6 SERVINGS

2 tablespoons olive oil
3 medium tomatoes, cut into
   small chunks
2 garlic cloves, minced
1 tablespoon chopped fresh
   basil
½ teaspoon dried thyme
1 teaspoon salt
½ teaspoon black pepper
3 medium yellow squash, cut
   into 1-inch chunks
2 medium zucchini, cut into 1-inch chunks

TIPS FROM THE PROS

This dish comes alive even more when topped with a sprinkle of grated Parmesan cheese just before serving.

Heat the oil in a large skillet over medium heat. Add the tomatoes, garlic, basil, thyme, salt, and pepper; cover and cook for 5 to 6 minutes, stirring occasionally. Add the yellow squash and zucchini; cover and cook for 10 minutes. Uncover and cook for 3 to 5 minutes, or until the vegetables are tender and the sauce has thickened slightly.

Old-fashioned Baked Beans

For true home-style baked beans, there are two steps you absolutely cannot skip. The blend must include a few strips of bacon, and the beans must be allowed to simmer for a long time. Remember, the longer they bake, the more flavor they'll have.

6 TO 8 SERVINGS

4 slices bacon, diced
2 cans (16 ounces each) baked beans
1 large onion, finely chopped
1½ cups ketchup
⅓ cup molasses
¼ cup (½ stick) butter, melted
2 tablespoons yellow mustard

Preheat the oven to 375°F. Coat a 9" × 13" baking dish with nonstick cooking spray. In a large skillet, cook the bacon over medium heat for 4 to 6 minutes, or until crisp, stirring frequently. Remove from the heat and add the remaining ingredients; mix well. Spoon into the baking dish and bake for 60 to 70 minutes, or until thickened and bubbly. Serve.

Creamy Coleslaw

Although you can buy ready-made coleslaw dressing in the supermarket, it's the real thing that makes all the difference. With this old-time favorite, the real thing is the buttermilk. That's what adds the extra-creamy touch.

6 TO 8 SERVINGS

½ cup mayonnaise
⅓ cup milk
1 teaspoon white vinegar
¼ cup sugar
1 tablespoon powdered dry
  buttermilk
¼ teaspoon salt
1 package (16 ounces) cabbage
  slaw mix (see Helpful
  Hints)

HELPFUL HINTS
This recipe is extra easy because you don't have to shred the cabbage yourself. Cabbage slaw mix can be found in the produce section of your supermarket next to the bagged salads. (Sometimes I add a shredded carrot to the mix.)

In a large bowl, whisk together all the ingredients except the cabbage slaw mix until smooth and creamy. Add the slaw mix and toss until well coated. Cover and chill for at least 1 hour before serving.

Rice Pilaf

Rice pilaf is one of my favorite side dishes. It can be made with any variety of steamed rice cooked in a meat, chicken, fish, or vegetable broth. I like to make it extra light and fluffy by adding some orzo pasta. This makes it as fine as any pilaf dish served at a four-star restaurant.

4 TO 6 SERVINGS

¼ cup (½ stick) butter
1 cup orzo pasta
1 large onion, chopped
1 can (14½ ounces) ready-to-
    use chicken broth
1 cup water
1 cup long-grain rice
¾ teaspoon salt
¼ teaspoon black pepper

TIPS FROM THE PROS

This looks great served with sliced scallions sprinkled over the top.

Melt the butter in a soup pot over medium heat. Add the orzo and onion and sauté for 6 to 8 minutes, or until the orzo is golden and the onion is tender. Add the remaining ingredients; mix well and bring to a boil. Reduce the heat to low, cover, and simmer for 30 to 35 minutes, or until no liquid remains. Fluff with a fork and serve.

Mediterranean-Style Couscous

Couscous isn't a tropical bird, it's a pasta-like dish often studded with diced veggies. Although it's primarily found in Moroccan and Middle Eastern restaurants, now you can find it right in your own kitchen, too.

5 TO 6 SERVINGS

2 tablespoons olive oil
1 small onion, finely chopped
1 carrot, diced
1 small zucchini, diced
2 garlic cloves, minced
1 can (14½ ounces) ready-to-
   use chicken broth
¼ cup water
½ teaspoon salt
1 package (10 ounces)
   couscous

HELPFUL HINTS

One of the best known regional dishes from North Africa, couscous is a staple in that area. The word *couscous* refers both to the plain grain itself and to the dish made of the grain combined with chunks of chicken, meat, and/or vegetables.

Heat the oil in a large saucepan over medium-high heat. Add the onion, carrot, zucchini, and garlic and sauté for 10 to 12 minutes, or until tender. Add the broth, water, and salt and bring to a boil. Stir in the couscous; cover and remove from the heat. Allow to sit, covered, for 5 minutes. Fluff with a fork and serve.

Yorkshire Pudding

English pubs are known for dishes like shepherd's pie, fish and chips, and Yorkshire pudding, a popover-like side dish. Yorkshire pudding is a super go-along for juicy prime rib, and I like to prepare mine muffin-style so that everyone can enjoy his or her very own "pudding."

6 SERVINGS

2 cold eggs
1 cup cold milk
1 tablespoon butter, melted
1 cup all-purpose flour
½ teaspoon salt

HELPFUL HINTS

Serve these hot with butter. They disappear really fast, so I suggest making a double batch!

Preheat the oven to 425°F. Coat a 6-cup muffin tin with nonstick cooking spray. In a large bowl, combine all the ingredients, mixing with a spoon until just blended (a few lumps may remain). Immediately pour into the muffin cups, filling each cup three-quarters full. Bake for 30 to 35 minutes, or until golden and puffy. Remove from the muffin tin and serve immediately.

Lyonnaise Potatoes

There's really nothing to this fancy-sounding side dish but a few ingredients and a little cooking time. Oh, what the onion does for these potatoes!

4 TO 6 SERVINGS

4 large potatoes, peeled and
    cut into ⅛-inch-thick slices
1 large onion, thinly sliced
½ cup (1 stick) butter, melted
½ teaspoon paprika
1 teaspoon salt
½ teaspoon black pepper

TIPS FROM THE PROS

Serve on a platter, sprinkled with a little more paprika for an extra-fancy look.

In a medium bowl, toss the potatoes and onion with the remaining ingredients until well coated. Place the mixture in a large skillet, cover, and cook over medium-low heat for about 30 minutes, or until the potatoes are fork-tender and slightly browned, turning occasionally with a spatula.

Smashed Potatoes

Smashed potatoes may be a popular restaurant item these days, but they were created out of convenience more than anything else. Instead of spending hours peeling potatoes for mashing, many restaurants started mashing them, skins and all, with garlic, onions, or both, and voilà! Smashed potatoes were born.

6 TO 8 SERVINGS

4 pounds red potatoes,
    scrubbed and quartered
½ cup (1 stick) butter
1 cup sour cream
¼ cup milk
½ teaspoon garlic powder
½ teaspoon onion powder
1½ teaspoons salt
1 teaspoon black pepper

TIPS FROM THE PROS

If you like smooth smashed potatoes, after mixing everything together, whip them with an electric beater. And for extra crunch, sprinkle some canned French-fried onions over the top.

Place the potatoes in a soup pot and add enough water to cover them. Bring to a boil over high heat, then reduce the heat to medium and cook for 15 to 20 minutes, or until the potatoes are fork-tender; drain and place in a large bowl. Add the remaining ingredients and "smash" the potatoes with a potato masher until the desired consistency, leaving some potato chunks. Serve immediately, or place in a casserole dish and keep warm in a 250°F. oven for up to an hour before serving.

Sizzling Home Fries

The best home fries are still the ones made in diners—you know, the places that are nicknamed "greasy spoons." There's just something special about the taste of potatoes slung around a sizzling-hot grill and mixed with the flavors of eggs and bacon that can't be beat. Wait until you try these—they're a breakfast (or anytime) winner.

4 TO 6 SERVINGS

2 teaspoons paprika
1 teaspoon garlic powder
1 teaspoon salt
½ teaspoon black pepper
6 red potatoes (about 2½ pounds), scrubbed and cut into 1-inch
   chunks
2 medium onions, chopped
⅓ cup vegetable oil

In a large bowl, combine the paprika, garlic powder, salt, and pepper; mix well. Add the potatoes and onions; toss to coat evenly. Heat the oil in a large skillet over medium-high heat. Add the potato mixture to the skillet, cover, and cook for 10 minutes. Increase the heat to high, uncover, and cook for 8 to 10 minutes, or until the potatoes are tender and golden, turning occasionally.

Parsleyed Red Potatoes

Once in a while, we're reminded that basic is best. And we sure can't go wrong with these lightly buttered tender potatoes. They're a long-time restaurant and home-style favorite.

4 TO 6 SERVINGS

> 2 quarts water
> 1 onion, quartered
> 2 teaspoons salt
> 2 pounds (about 20) small red new potatoes, washed
> ¼ cup (½ stick) butter
> 1 garlic clove, minced
> ¼ cup chopped fresh parsley

In a soup pot, bring the water, onion, and salt to a boil over high heat. Using a potato peeler, peel off a strip around the center of each potato. Place the potatoes in the pot, cover, and cook for 12 to 15 minutes, or just until fork-tender; drain well in a colander and keep warm. Melt the butter in the same pot over medium heat. Add the garlic and sauté for 1 to 2 minutes, or until tender. Stir in the parsley, then return the potatoes to the pot and toss to coat evenly. Serve immediately.

Stuffed Baked Potatoes

Looking for a satisfying side dish? This version of the "hoo hoo–fancy" restaurant favorite really fits the bill.

6 SERVINGS

6 large baking potatoes
2 eggs
1 cup sour cream
½ cup (1 stick) butter, softened
½ teaspoon onion powder
½ teaspoon salt
¼ teaspoon black pepper
Paprika for sprinkling

TIPS FROM THE PROS

For a fancy look, pipe the potato mixture into the potato shells using a pastry bag or a resealable plastic storage bag with a bottom corner snipped off.

Preheat the oven to 400°F. Scrub the potatoes and pierce them several times with a fork. Bake for 1 hour, or until fork-tender; leave the oven on. Slice about ½ inch off the top of each potato and scoop out the pulp, leaving about a ¼-inch-thick potato shell; place the pulp in a medium bowl. Add the eggs, sour cream, butter, onion powder, salt, and pepper; beat until smooth. Spoon into the potato shells and sprinkle the tops lightly with paprika. Bake for 25 to 30 minutes, or until the potatoes begin to brown on top. Serve immediately.

Potato Pancakes

The secret to making the crispiest potato pancakes is to squeeze as much water as possible from the potatoes and onions after shredding. If you've got watery batter, you're gonna have soggy pancakes.

6 TO 7 PANCAKES

1½ pounds potatoes, peeled
  and shredded
1 small onion, finely chopped
1 egg, beaten
½ cup all-purpose flour
1 teaspoon baking powder
¾ teaspoon salt
½ teaspoon black pepper
Vegetable oil for frying

TIPS FROM THE PROS

These are usually served with toppers such as sour cream and applesauce.

Place the potatoes and onion in a fine strainer. Press down on the mixture with the back of a large spoon to extract excess moisture. (If still watery, wrap them in a clean dish towel and squeeze firmly.) In a large bowl, combine the potatoes and onion, egg, flour, baking powder, salt, and pepper; mix well. In a large deep skillet, heat about ¼ inch of oil over medium-high heat. Add the batter in batches by ¼-cupfuls to the skillet and flatten gently with a spatula to form pancakes, being careful not to crowd the skillet. Fry until the pancakes are golden on both sides, turning once. (If you like them crisper, fry until they're flecked with brown.) Drain on a paper towel–lined platter and serve hot.

Baked Sweet Potato Fries

Most of us prepare sweet potatoes one way: baked. I mean, that's the favorite way most of us have always enjoyed them. For me, that changed when I tried the sweet potato fries at a little restaurant/ice cream parlor my family frequents. One bite and I was hooked . . . you will be, too!

4 TO 6 SERVINGS

4 large sweet potatoes (about 2 pounds), peeled and cut lengthwise into ½-inch-thick strips

⅓ cup vegetable oil

½ teaspoon salt

TIPS FROM THE PROS

As an alternative to salt, you might want to try sprinkling your sweet potato fries with a cinnamon-sugar mix, or drizzling them with some warm maple syrup. Mmm, mmm!

Preheat the oven to 450°F. In a large bowl, combine the potatoes and oil; toss to coat completely. Spoon the potatoes onto rimmed baking sheets in a single layer and bake for 15 to 18 minutes, or until golden. Turn the potatoes over and bake for 5 to 8 minutes, or until golden. Drain on a paper towel–lined platter. Sprinkle the sweet potato fries with the salt and serve.

DESSERTS

Overstuffed Napoleons

Let's leave the homemade puff pastry to the pastry chefs and use the shortcut packaged variety to make these easy-as-can-be napoleons. I mean, why should we spend time making flaky dough from scratch when we can use a convenience item that gives us extra time to enjoy this classic sweet treat?!

12 TO 16 SERVINGS

1 package (17¼ ounces) frozen puff pastry (2 sheets), thawed
2 packages (4 servings each) instant vanilla pudding and pie filling
1¾ cups milk, divided
1 container (8 ounces) frozen whipped topping, thawed
2 cups confectioners' sugar
¼ teaspoon unsweetened cocoa

Preheat the oven to 400°F. Bake the puff pastry sheets according to the package directions; allow to cool. In a medium bowl, combine the pudding mix and 1½ cups milk. Whisk until thickened, then fold in the whipped topping. Spread the mixture over 1 layer of puff pastry. Place the other puff pastry layer flat side up over the pudding. Using a cookie sheet, press down lightly to distribute the pudding evenly and level the pastry just until the filling begins to ooze out the sides. Combine the confectioners' sugar and the remaining ¼ cup milk; mix well to make a glaze. Reserve 2 tablespoons of the glaze in a small bowl; spread the remaining glaze over the top of the napoleon. Stir the cocoa into the reserved glaze; mix well and drizzle over the glazed napoleon. Chill for at least 3 hours, until set, before serving. Carefully cut into serving-sized pieces with a serrated knife.

Bakery-Style Éclairs

*Every once in a while we just might want to spend a little extra time prepar-
ing an amazing dessert for a special occasion. Well, when it comes to éclairs,
believe me, there's nothing like homemade. Sure, we can pick up some
chocolate éclairs at the bakery or supermarket, but when they're this easy to
make . . . why bother?*

10 ÉCLAIRS

1 cup water
½ cup (1 stick) butter, cut into quarters
¼ teaspoon salt
1 cup all-purpose flour
4 eggs, at room temperature
2 cups (1 pint) heavy cream
1 package (4-serving size) instant vanilla pudding and pie filling
1½ cups confectioners' sugar
3 tablespoons unsweetened cocoa
2 tablespoons milk

Preheat the oven to 400°F. In a medium saucepan, bring the water,
butter, and salt to a boil over medium-high heat. Add the flour all at
once and stir quickly with a wooden spoon until the mixture forms a
ball; remove from the heat. Add 1 egg to the mixture and beat hard
with the wooden spoon to blend. Add the remaining eggs one at a
time, beating well after each addition; each egg must be completely
blended before the next egg is added. As you beat the dough, its consistency will change from looking almost curdled to smooth. When it
is smooth, spoon the dough into a large resealable plastic storage bag
and, using scissors, snip off one bottom corner of the bag, making a

1-inch-long cut. Gently squeeze the bag to form ten 1" × 4" dough logs about 2 inches apart on a large ungreased rimmed baking sheet. Bake for 40 to 45 minutes, until golden and puffy. Remove to a wire rack to cool. In a large bowl, beat the cream until stiff peaks form. Fold in the pudding mix and set aside. In a small bowl, stir together the confectioners' sugar, cocoa, and milk to make a smooth icing. Cut the éclair shells horizontally in half and spoon the pudding mixture equally into the bottoms. Replace the tops of the éclair shells and spread the cocoa icing over the tops. Cover loosely and chill for at least 1 hour before serving.

Melt-in-Your-Mouth Tiramisù

Save room for this light and creamy version of the classic Italian specialty!

6 TO 8 SERVINGS

1 cup warm water
4 teaspoons instant coffee granules
¼ cup coffee-flavored liqueur
½ teaspoon vanilla extract
1 container (8 ounces)
  mascarpone cheese
  (see Helpful Hints)
½ cup sugar
1 cup (½ pint) heavy cream
2 packages (3 ounces each)
  ladyfingers
½ teaspoon unsweetened cocoa

HELPFUL HINTS

Mascarpone cheese is a buttery-smooth Italian cheese often found in supermarket deli departments. If it's not available, you can substitute cream cheese beaten with a little milk until creamy and smooth.

In a small bowl, combine the water, coffee granules, liqueur, and vanilla; stir to dissolve the coffee, then set aside. In a large bowl, beat the mascarpone cheese and sugar until smooth; set aside. In a medium bowl, beat the heavy cream until stiff peaks form. Fold half of the whipped cream into the cheese mixture until thoroughly combined. Line the bottom of an 8-inch square baking dish with 1 package of ladyfingers, slightly overlapping to fit. Spoon half of the coffee mixture over them, then half of the cheese mixture. Top with the remaining package of ladyfingers and repeat the layering with the coffee and cheese mixtures. Spoon the remaining whipped cream over the top and sprinkle with the cocoa. Cover and chill for at least 3 hours before serving.

New York Cheesecake

The most famous of all New York–style cheesecakes comes from Lindy's Restaurant. People flock from all over to taste bite after creamy bite of their luscious cheesecake. Luckily for us, we can sample this similar version without leaving our kitchens.

12 TO 16 SERVINGS

1 cup plus 2 tablespoons all-purpose flour, divided
1½ cups sugar, divided
½ cup (1 stick) butter, softened
2 egg yolks
Grated peel of 1 lemon, divided
3 packages (8 ounces each) cream cheese, softened
½ teaspoon vanilla extract
3 eggs
¼ cup milk
¼ teaspoon salt

Preheat the oven to 450°F. In a large bowl, combine 1 cup flour, ¼ cup sugar, the butter, 1 egg yolk, and half the lemon peel; mix well and press into the bottom and up the sides of a 9-inch springform pan. In a large bowl, beat the cream cheese, vanilla, and the remaining lemon peel until smooth. Add the remaining 1¼ cups sugar, 2 tablespoons flour, and egg yolk, the whole eggs, milk, and salt; beat until smooth. Pour into the crust and bake for 15 minutes; reduce the heat to 300°F. and bake for 55 to 60 minutes more, or until the center is set. Remove from the oven and allow to cool for 1 hour. Cover and chill overnight before serving.

Triple Chocolate Cake

You know how some diners have the biggest cakes you've ever seen displayed in beautifully lit cases so your taste buds start working from the minute you walk in? One of their offerings is almost always mile-high chocolate cake, so, of course, I had to include an extra-chocolatey chocolate cake recipe in this collection of restaurant favorites.

12 TO 16 SERVINGS

1 package (18½ ounces) chocolate cake mix
1 package (4-serving size) instant chocolate pudding and pie filling
½ cup sour cream
½ cup vegetable oil
4 eggs
1 cup water
1 cup heavy cream
1 container (16 ounces) milk chocolate frosting

Preheat the oven to 350°F. Coat two 9-inch round cake pans with nonstick cooking spray. In a large bowl, combine the cake mix, pudding mix, sour cream, oil, eggs, and water; mix well. Divide the batter evenly between the cake pans. Bake for 35 to 40 minutes, or until a toothpick inserted in the center comes out clean. Allow to cool slightly, then remove to a wire rack to cool completely. Meanwhile, in a medium bowl, beat the heavy cream until stiff peaks form. Add half of the frosting; mix well. Chill the filling until the cake is cooled. Place one cake layer on a serving platter; spread with the filling. Place the second cake layer over the first and frost the top and sides with the remaining frosting. Serve immediately, or chill until ready to serve.

Black Forest Cake

A dessert menu might use terms like rich *and* ruby red cherries *to describe this tasty treat. I describe it in two words: absolutely awesome!*

12 TO 16 SERVINGS

1 package (18¼ ounces)
    devil's food cake mix

3 eggs

¾ cup water

½ cup vegetable oil

1 can (21 ounces) cherry pie
    filling, drained, with ½ cup
    sauce reserved

1 cup (½ pint) heavy cream

3 tablespoons confectioners' sugar

1 container (16 ounces) chocolate frosting

TIPS FROM THE PROS

For that elegant finishing touch, top the cake with chocolate curls and additional cherries or chocolate-covered cherries.

Preheat the oven to 350°F. Coat two 9-inch round cake pans with nonstick cooking spray. In a medium bowl, combine the cake mix, eggs, water, oil, and the reserved ½ cup cherry sauce; mix well. Divide the batter evenly between the cake pans. Bake for 30 to 35 minutes, or until a wooden toothpick inserted in the center comes out clean. Allow to cool for 10 minutes, then invert onto wire racks to cool completely. Beat the heavy cream until stiff peaks form; beat in the confectioners' sugar. Place 1 cooled cake layer upside down on a serving platter and cover the top with half of the whipped cream; scatter the cherries over the whipped cream. Place the second cake layer over the first and frost the sides with the chocolate frosting. Frost the top with the remaining whipped cream. Serve, or cover loosely and chill until ready to serve.

Buttermilk Carrot Cake

Shy away from using buttermilk in recipes because you think it's high in fat? In fact, the opposite is true. So why not give buttermilk a try, especially since it adds an extra-creamy touch to our favorite desserts.

12 TO 16 SERVINGS

2 cups all-purpose flour
2 teaspoons baking powder
2 teaspoons baking soda
1 tablespoon ground cinnamon
½ teaspoon ground allspice
½ teaspoon salt
1 pound carrots, shredded (about 2 cups packed)
1 can (8 ounces) crushed pineapple, drained
2 cups packed light brown sugar
1 cup finely chopped walnuts
4 eggs
½ cup buttermilk
½ cup vegetable oil
Buttery Cream Cheese Frosting (opposite page)

Preheat the oven to 350°F. Coat two 9-inch round cake pans with nonstick cooking spray. In a medium bowl, combine the flour, baking powder, baking soda, cinnamon, allspice, and salt. In a large bowl, combine the remaining ingredients except the frosting. Add the flour mixture; mix well. Divide the batter evenly into the cake pans. Bake for 35 to 40 minutes, until a toothpick inserted in the center comes out clean. Cool for 10 minutes, then invert onto wire racks to cool completely. Place 1 cake layer upside down on a serving plate; frost the top. Place the second layer upside down over the first; frost the top and sides. Cover loosely and chill for at least 3 hours before serving.

Buttery Cream Cheese Frosting

Carrot cake just isn't carrot cake unless it's topped with loads of cream cheese frosting. Here's one you'll find yourself using again and again, 'cause it works on almost any cake.

ABOUT 1 ¼ CUPS

1 package (8 ounces)
    cream cheese, softened
½ cup (1 stick) unsalted
    butter, softened
2 cups confectioners'
    sugar

TIPS FROM THE PROS

Top the frosted cake with a little grated carrot for that professional look.

In a large bowl, beat the cream cheese and butter until creamy. Gradually add the confectioners' sugar, beating for 1 to 2 minutes, until smooth. Use immediately, or cover and chill until ready to use. Bring to room temperature before using.

Creamy Rice Pudding

To make creamy-style rice pudding, you need to bake it for about an hour. So, with this recipe, the hardest part is waiting for that first spoonful!

8 TO 10 SERVINGS

¼ cup (½ stick) butter, softened
1 cup sugar
4 eggs
3 cups (1½ pints) half-and-half
2 cups cooked rice
½ cup raisins
1 teaspoon vanilla extract
½ teaspoon ground cinnamon
¼ teaspoon salt

Preheat the oven to 350°F. Coat a 1½-quart casserole dish with nonstick cooking spray. In a large bowl, cream the butter and sugar. Add the eggs one at a time, beating after each addition until well combined. Add the remaining ingredients; mix well. Pour into the casserole dish and bake for 55 to 60 minutes, or until the top is golden (the pudding will be loose). Serve warm, or cover and chill for at least 4 hours before serving.

Strawberry Parfaits

When I was growing up, the selection of restaurants was nowhere near as big as it is today. In fact, I remember a time when the only restaurants around were luncheonettes. My favorite one made the yummiest parfaits, and now I've re-created them for you.

4 SERVINGS

1 package (4-serving size)
   strawberry-flavored gelatin
1 cup boiling water
½ cup cold water
1 cup frozen whipped topping,
   thawed

TIPS FROM THE PROS

Make your parfaits really stand out by topping them with big juicy red strawberries.

In an 8-inch square baking dish, dissolve the gelatin in the boiling water. Stir in the cold water; cover and chill until firm. Cut into 1-inch cubes; place half of the cubes in 4 parfait glasses. Spoon half of the whipped topping into the glasses, followed by the remaining gelatin cubes; top with the remaining whipped topping. Serve immediately, or cover loosely and chill until ready to serve.

Rich Chocolate Mousse

Are you one of those people who thinks that chocolate mousse is a fancy dish that takes hours and hours to make? Boy, are you gonna be surprised when you find out how easy it is to make at home.

6 TO 8 SERVINGS

1 cup (6 ounces) semisweet
   chocolate chips
2 cups (1 pint) heavy cream,
   divided
1 tablespoon confectioners'
   sugar

TIPS FROM THE PROS

Wow the gang even more by garnishing this with additional real whipped cream and some shaved chocolate.

In a medium saucepan, combine the chocolate chips and ½ cup heavy cream over medium heat until the chocolate chips melt and the mixture is smooth, stirring constantly. Remove from the heat and allow to cool. In a medium bowl, beat the remaining 1½ cups heavy cream and the confectioners' sugar until stiff peaks form. Gently fold the chocolate mixture into the whipped cream until well blended (do not stir). Cover and chill for at least 1 hour before serving.

Crème Brûlée

There are many different stories about the origins of this custardy caramel dessert. Lots of chefs and restaurants claim they invented the specialty that's now served in so many fancy restaurants. When you really want to pull out all the stops with something homemade—you can.

6 SERVINGS

2 cups (1 pint) heavy cream
½ cup milk
1 cup sugar, divided
6 egg yolks
1 teaspoon vanilla extract

TIPS FROM THE PROS

These can be topped with the melted sugar and chilled for up to 2 hours before serving.

In a large saucepan, combine the heavy cream, milk, ½ cup sugar, the egg yolks, and vanilla over medium heat and cook for 30 minutes, stirring frequently; be careful not to boil. Remove from the heat and beat for 5 to 6 minutes, or until smooth and thick. Pour equally into six 1-cup custard cups. Chill for 4 to 6 hours, or until the custard is very firm. In a medium skillet, melt the remaining ½ cup sugar over medium heat until golden, then pour over the chilled custards; allow to chill for 15 to 20 minutes, or until the sugar hardens. Serve.

Poached Pears

Ever eat a big meal and think you're so stuffed that you couldn't possibly eat another bite? There's always room for this tasty but light sweet ending.

6 SERVINGS

2 cups apple juice
1 cup water
1 cup cinnamon red-hot
   candies
¾ cup sugar
2 tablespoons fresh lemon
   juice
6 firm ripe pears, peeled, with
   stems intact (see Tips from
   the Pros)
¼ cup apple jelly

TIPS FROM THE PROS

If you'd like, cut a thin slice off the bottom of the pears before cooking so they'll stand up straight for serving.

In a soup pot, combine the apple juice, water, cinnamon candies, sugar, and lemon juice over high heat; cook until the candy is dissolved, stirring occasionally. Add the pears; reduce the heat to medium-low, cover, and simmer for 25 to 30 minutes, or until soft, turning occasionally. Remove the pears to a bowl and reserve. Increase the heat to medium-high; add the apple jelly and boil for 10 minutes, or until slightly thickened. Spoon over the pears and allow to cool for 30 minutes. Serve warm, or cover and chill until ready to serve.

Piled-High Apple Pie

Apple pie is an all-American dish that's served everywhere from four-star gourmet restaurants to mom-and-pop diners. Not only is it a restaurant classic, but it's a great-tasting homemade family-pleaser, too.

6 TO 8 SERVINGS

¾ cup plus 1 teaspoon sugar, divided
1⅛ teaspoons ground
   cinnamon, divided
8 medium cooking apples,
   peeled, cored, and quartered
2 tablespoons all-purpose flour
1 tablespoon plus 2 teaspoons
   butter, softened
1 teaspoon lemon juice
1 package (15 ounces)
   refrigerated folded pie crusts

TIPS FROM THE PROS

Baking the pie on a cookie sheet minimizes oven cleanup if the filling should happen to bubble up out of the crust.

Preheat the oven to 425°F. In a small bowl, combine 1 teaspoon sugar and ⅛ teaspoon cinnamon; mix well and set aside. In a large bowl, combine the apples, flour, 1 tablespoon butter, the lemon juice, and the remaining ¾ cup sugar and 1 teaspoon cinnamon; toss to coat the apples well. Unfold 1 pie crust and place in a 9-inch pie plate, pressing the crust firmly against the plate. Pour the apple mixture into the pie crust, then place the remaining pie crust over the top. Trim and pinch the edges together to seal, fluting if desired. Using a sharp knife, cut four 1-inch slits in the top. Melt the remaining 2 teaspoons butter and brush over the top of the crust, then sprinkle with the cinnamon-sugar mixture. Bake on a cookie sheet for 45 to 50 minutes, or until the crust is golden.

Fresh Strawberry Pie

Cornstarch is one of those magical ingredients that most chefs and home cooks can't live without. It thickens gravies and soups, and it can be added to batters for better coating. I like its role in this recipe, 'cause it helps get the filling to just the perfect consistency.

6 TO 8 SERVINGS

One 9-inch frozen ready-to-bake deep-dish pie shell, thawed
4 pints fresh strawberries, washed and hulled, divided
¾ cup sugar
3 tablespoons cornstarch
½ cup water
⅛ teaspoon red food color

TIPS FROM THE PROS

Wanna make your gang really go crazy? Top your pie slices with dollops of fresh whipped cream.

Bake the pie shell according to the package directions; allow to cool. In a medium saucepan, combine 1 pint strawberries with the sugar and cook over medium heat, crushing the strawberries with the back of a spoon, until the mixture is thickened and syrupy. In a small bowl, whisk together the cornstarch and water until the cornstarch is dissolved, then add to the strawberry mixture. Cook for 2 to 3 minutes, or until the mixture is thickened, stirring frequently. Remove from the heat, add the food color, and mix until well blended; allow to cool completely, then place in a large bowl. Add the remaining whole strawberries and mix until the strawberries are well coated. Spoon into the pie shell, cover loosely, and chill for at least 2 hours before serving.

Bubbling Blueberry Cobbler

A basic cobbler consists of cooked fruit with some type of biscuit-like topping. Depending on what part of the country you're in, the fruit will vary, but one thing never changes—the old-fashioned good taste.

9 TO 12 SERVINGS

2 pints fresh blueberries,
    washed
⅔ cup sugar, divided
1¾ cups all-purpose flour,
    divided
¼ cup orange juice
½ cup heavy cream
¼ cup (½ stick) butter,
    softened
2 teaspoons baking powder
½ teaspoon salt

TIPS FROM THE PROS

Not blueberry season? Not to worry—just use two 12-ounce packages of frozen blueberries. The best part? There's no need to thaw them first!

Preheat the oven to 400°F. Coat a 9" × 13" baking dish with nonstick cooking spray. In a large bowl, combine the blueberries, ⅓ cup sugar, ¼ cup flour, and the orange juice; mix well and pour into the baking dish. In a medium bowl, combine the remaining 1½ cups flour and ⅓ cup sugar, the cream, butter, baking powder, and salt; mix until crumbly. Sprinkle over the blueberries. Bake for 25 to 30 minutes, or until the top is golden and the blueberry mixture is bubbly. Serve warm.

Mocha Mud Pie

The original mud pie hails from Mississippi, but now we find it served all over the country. It's one of those desserts you just can't say no to.

6 TO 8 SERVINGS

1 pint chocolate ice cream, softened
One 9-inch chocolate graham cracker pie crust
1 jar (11¾ ounces) hot fudge sauce, warmed, divided
1 pint coffee ice cream, softened
2 tablespoons chopped almonds

Spread the chocolate ice cream in the crust. Cover with about 1 cup of the hot fudge sauce, then cover and freeze for about 2 hours, or until firm. Spread the coffee ice cream over the frozen pie, then rewarm the remaining fudge sauce and drizzle it over the top. Sprinkle with the almonds, cover, and freeze for at least 2 hours before serving. Remove from the freezer 5 minutes before serving to allow the filling to soften slightly.

Jazzy Bananas Foster

Did you know that your kitchen can provide the flavor and feel of a New Orleans restaurant in a matter of minutes? Just grab a skillet and you'll be on your way to some jazzy good taste.

4 TO 6 SERVINGS

¼ cup (½ stick) butter
½ cup packed brown sugar
⅛ teaspoon ground cinnamon
3 medium bananas, peeled and sliced
¼ cup light or dark rum
1 quart vanilla ice cream

Melt the butter in a large skillet over medium heat. Add the brown sugar and cinnamon; stir until the sugar is melted. Stir in the bananas and rum; cook for 2 to 3 minutes, or until heated through. Scoop the ice cream into serving bowls and top with the banana mixture. Serve immediately.

Not-Fried "Fried" Ice Cream

Yes, they really do deep-fry ice cream in Mexican restaurants. And since that tends to get a little messy, go ahead and try this version. It's easier and neater, but just as tasty.

8 SERVINGS

1 quart vanilla ice cream
2½ cups oven-toasted corn
   cereal, coarsely crushed
1 tablespoon butter, melted
2 tablespoons sugar
1 teaspoon ground cinnamon

TIPS FROM THE PROS

It's nice to serve these in sundae glasses, each topped with caramel-flavor ice cream sauce, whipped cream, and a cherry. If you want to make this lighter, reduced-fat ice cream or frozen yogurt works just as well . . . and the way the coating is done, it still tastes just like it's been deep-fried.

Line a rimmed baking sheet with waxed paper. With a large spoon or an ice cream scoop, form the ice cream into 8 balls, each about 2½ inches in diameter. Place on the baking sheet, then place in the freezer for about 1 hour. Meanwhile, preheat the oven to 350°F. Coat another large rimmed baking sheet with nonstick cooking spray. In a medium bowl, combine the remaining ingredients; mix well and spread on the baking sheet. Bake for 5 to 7 minutes, or until lightly browned and crisp. Remove to a shallow dish and allow to cool completely. Line another rimmed baking sheet with waxed paper. Remove the ice cream balls from the freezer and roll in the cereal mixture, coating on all sides. Place on the baking sheet and freeze for 2 to 3 hours, or until the ice cream is firm; serve immediately, or cover and keep frozen until ready to serve.

A

B

C

D

E

F

G

H

I

J

K

L

M

N

O

P

Mr. Food®'s Library Gives You More Ways to Say. . . "OOH IT'S SO GOOD!!®"

WILLIAM MORROW

Mr. Food From My Kitchen to Yours: Stories and Recipes from Home

Q

Easy Tex-Mex

R

Mr. Food One Pot, One Meal More than one million copies of Mr. Food cookbooks sold!

S

Mr. Food COOL CRAVINGS

T

Mr. Food's Italian Kitchen Quick, Easy, and Fun Recipes!

U

Mr. Food's Simple Southern Favorites

V

A Mr. Food Christmas Homemade and Hassle-Free

W

Mr. Food Cooking by the Calendar Fifty-two Weeks of Year-Round Favorites

X

Mr. Food's Meals in Minutes Quick, Easy, Fun Recipes!

Y

Mr. Food's GOOD TIMES, GOOD FOOD COOKBOOK Tempting Tastes of Yesterday and Today

Z

Mr. Food's Restaurant Favorites Easy as Can Be!

AA

Mr. Food ® CAN HELP YOU BE A KITCHEN HERO!

Let **Mr. Food** ® make your life easier with Quick, No-Fuss Recipes and Helpful Kitchen Tips for

Family Dinners • Soups and Salads • Potluck Dishes • Barbecues • Special Brunches • Unbelievable Desserts

. . . and that's just the beginning!

Complete your **Mr. Food** ® cookbook library today. It's so simple to share in all the **"OOH IT'S SO GOOD!!®"**

✂ -

TITLE	PRICE		QUANTITY		
A. **Mr. Food** ® Cooks Like Mama	@ $14.95 each	x	_____	=	$_____
B. The **Mr. Food** ® Cookbook, *OOH IT'S SO GOOD!!*®	@ $14.95 each	x	_____	=	$_____
C. **Mr. Food** ® Cooks Chicken	@ $ 9.95 each	x	_____	=	$_____
D. **Mr. Food** ® Cooks Pasta	@ $11.95 each	x	_____	=	$_____
E. **Mr. Food** ® Makes Dessert	@ $ 9.95 each	x	_____	=	$_____
F. **Mr. Food** ® Cooks Real American	@ $14.95 each	x	_____	=	$_____
G. **Mr. Food** ®'s Favorite Cookies	@ $11.95 each	x	_____	=	$_____
H. **Mr. Food** ®'s Quick and Easy Side Dishes	@ $11.95 each	x	_____	=	$_____
I. **Mr. Food** ® Grills It All in a Snap	@ $11.95 each	x	_____	=	$_____
J. **Mr. Food** ®'s Fun Kitchen Tips and Shortcuts (and Recipes, Too!)	@ $11.95 each	x	_____	=	$_____
K. **Mr. Food** ®'s Old World Cooking Made Easy	@ $14.95 each	x	_____	=	$_____
L. "Help, **Mr. Food** ®! Company's Coming!"	@ $14.95 each	x	_____	=	$_____
M. **Mr. Food** ® Pizza 1-2-3	@ $12.00 each	x	_____	=	$_____
N. **Mr. Food** ® Meal Around the Table	@ $12.00 each	x	_____	=	$_____
O. **Mr. Food** ® Simply Chocolate	@ $12.00 each	x	_____	=	$_____
P. **Mr. Food** ® A Little Lighter	@ $14.95 each	x	_____	=	$_____
Q. **Mr. Food** ® From My Kitchen to Yours: Stories and Recipes from Home	@ $14.95 each	x	_____	=	$_____
R. **Mr. Food** ® Easy Tex-Mex	@ $11.95 each	x	_____	=	$_____
S. **Mr. Food** ® One Pot, One Meal	@ $11.95 each	x	_____	=	$_____
T. **Mr. Food** ® Cool Cravings: Easy Chilled and Frozen Desserts	@ $11.95 each	x	_____	=	$_____
U. **Mr. Food** ®'s Italian Kitchen	@ $14.95 each	x	_____	=	$_____
V. **Mr. Food** ®'s Simple Southern Favorites	@ $14.95 each	x	_____	=	$_____
W. A **Mr. Food** ® Christmas: Homemade and Hassle-Free	@ $19.95 each	x	_____	=	$_____
X. **Mr. Food** ® Cooking by the Calendar	@ $14.95 each	x	_____	=	$_____
Y. **Mr. Food** ®'s Meals in Minutes	@ $14.95 each	x	_____	=	$_____
Z. **Mr. Food** ®'s Good Times, Good Food Cookbook	@ $14.95 each	x	_____	=	$_____
A A. **Mr. Food** ®'s Restaurant Favorites	@ $14.95 each	x	_____	=	$_____

Send payment to:
Mr. Food ®
P.O. Box 9227
Coral Springs, FL 33075-9227

Book Total	$	_____
+ Postage & Handling for *First Copy*	$	**4.00**
+$1 Postage & Handling for Ea. Add'l. Copy (Canadian Orders Add Add'l. $2.00 *Per Copy*)	$	_____

Name _____

Street _____ Apt._____

City _____ State_____ Zip_____
BKAA1

Method of Payment Enclosed ☐ Check or ☐ Money Order

Please allow up to 6 weeks for delivery.

Subtotal	$	_____
Add 6% Sales Tax (FL Residents Only)	$	_____
Total in U.S. Funds	$	_____